Tales of The Old River Rod and Gun,
Bloody Mary Society and Gentlemen's Club
and Other Stories

Tales of the OLD RIVER ROD AND GUN, BLOODY MARY SOCIETY AND GENTLEMEN'S CLUB and Other Stories

Bob McDill

Printed in the United States of America

Cover and Book Design by Gary Gore

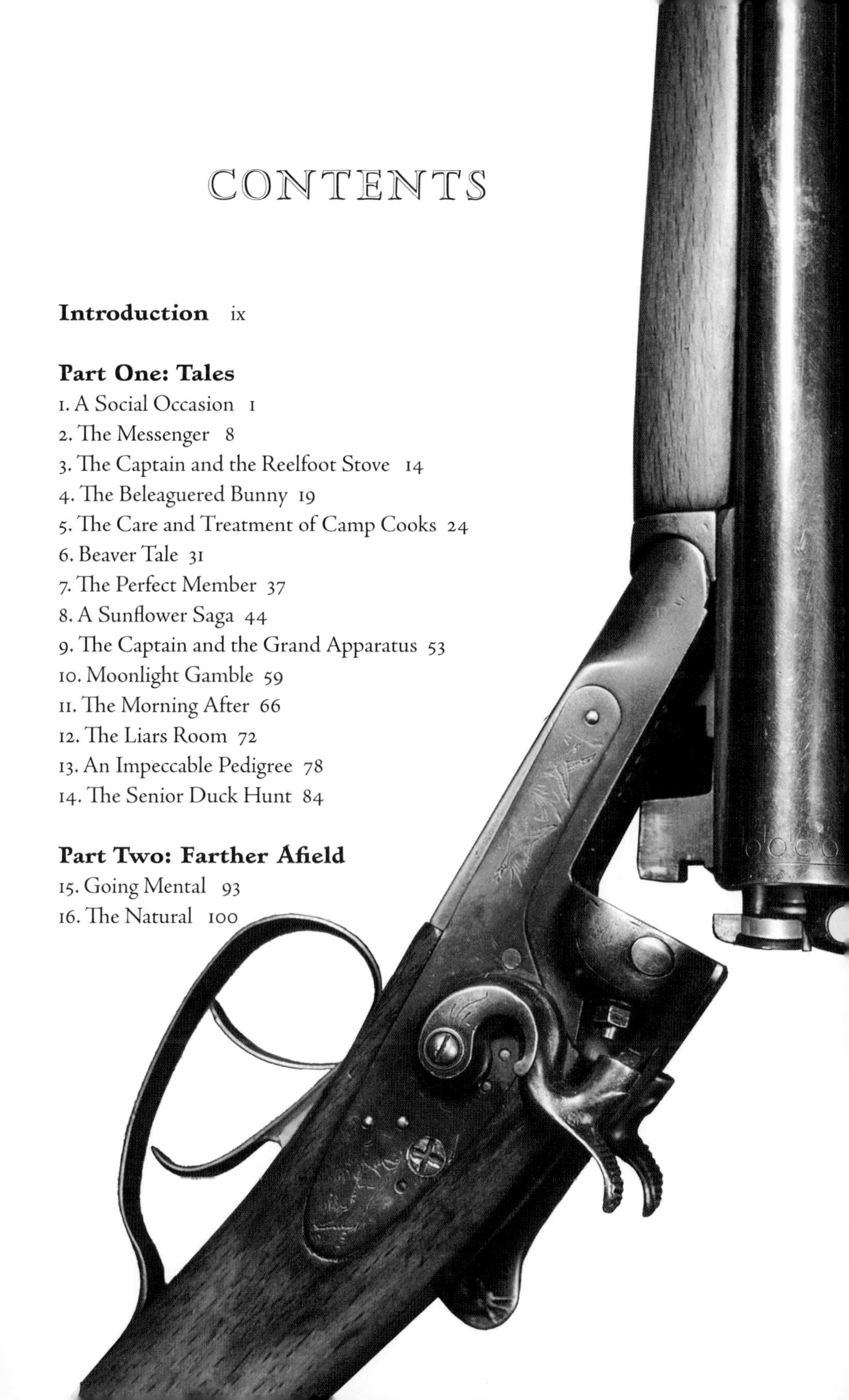

CONTENTS

Part Three: Way Far

Dedication

This book is dedicated to the following people:

First, to the friends and companions with whom
I've shared fields, woods, grouse moors, and duck blinds
throughout my life.

Second, to the members of
my hunting club in Squeeze Bottom, Tennessee.
A finer and more entertaining group of men
cannot be found.

Finally, to the guides, loaders, and game keepers
I've been fortunate to know and shoot with.
I thank them all for their excellent assistance
and unfailing good manners.

All of us have laughed together, celebrated together,
and huddled in frozen misery together.

INTRODUCTION

Friends have been asking me for years to put all these stories together in one place. In the past, they were handed around piecemeal from one reader to another either via well-worn copies of *Shooting Sportsman* or copies from my desktop printer. I hesitated for a long time, wondering at what point I might have enough for a full-length book. Then there was the question of not knowing if I had one more good story in me that might not be included. As far as the first concern, I reached that point some time ago. As for the second, there's always book 2.

Some characters in these stories are real people and mentioned by name. Others are completely made up. Still others are based on real people, but their names have been changed and their idiosyncrasies greatly exaggerated. So, if you see a person in these pages who is depicted as a fool and you think he might be based on you, don't call me. It isn't you. I made that one up.

For me, bird hunting began in my childhood, tramping the marshes around my home on the coast of Texas. Eventually it took me to distant places.

Some years the shooting was good. Other times birds were scarce as frog fur. But looking back, it was all a hell of a good time.

Special thanks to my two longtime editors and advisors, Katharine McDill Stover and Jennifer Kimball. Thank you, ladies, for your invaluable advice and support.

PART ONE

Tales

ALAN PHILLIPS

1

A Social Occasion

From *Shooting Sportsman*

In the South, September 1 does not necessarily signal the arrival of fall. True, a few leaves on the tupelo trees have turned blood red. The corn is plump, and on each ear, the silk hangs down brown and flaccid. But the temperature has moderated only a few degrees below its summer average. Autumn is still only a feeling, a promise. What gives the date significance is that as far back as anyone can remember, it's been the opening day of dove season. In the South, this approaches a national holiday. In small towns and rural areas, businesses close early. Khaki and camo clothes are worn from dawn until dusk, and no. 7 1/2 field loads appear on sale in every grocery store and gas station.

In our area, a dove hunt is more than a shoot. It's a social occasion. Some people bring picnics to the field. They arrive early and sit under the trees, lingering over lunch and waiting for the birds to fly in midafternoon. Parties often follow the hunt. If a good cook is on hand, he might prepare a dove dinner. The ladies might make decorations of autumn leaves to be placed on outdoor tables. A local boy might even be employed as a bartender. Invitations to good shoots are much sought after. If the favor can't be returned in kind, it is repaid with boxes of good cigars or bottles of fine whiskey.

At the Old River Rod and Gun, Bloody Mary Society and Gentlemen's Club, we usually put on just such a shindig. At least we tried. Some years the hunting was good. Other times, in spite of all our best efforts, birds were scarce as frog fur. This year, however, promised to be a barn burner. I had witnessed hundreds of doves feeding and trading in the field the afternoon before opening day, and I was determined to shoot my share. This year I would get serious.

The afternoon started out fine. I arrived in the field about 2:30, giving myself plenty of time. If the birds flew, they usually flew between three and six o'clock. Experience told me that at six, they disappeared just as if someone had shut a big door somewhere across the river. Aside from the fact that I had left my wristwatch draped over the gearshift of my Jeep, something I would later regret, everything had gone according to plan. Soon my stool was set up in what I knew to be a pretty good spot. My water jug was stowed underneath, my shell bag was open, and my little Birmingham 20 gauge was resting across my knees. My meat gun. I wasn't fooling around. I settled in to wait for the sun to sink a bit. Then the trouble began.

"Oh, Bob! Come over here a minute!" someone called out.

I looked up and saw Bill and Margaret Goodheart shouting and waving at me. They were stationed about 100 yards up the tractor road in the shade of a bur oak. I had always liked the Goodhearts. Why not pay them a little visit? After all, there was plenty of time. I laid my shotgun carefully across my stool and strolled up the lane. There they sat in two cushy chairs. Between them were an ice chest, a half empty picnic basket, a thermos, and a pile of scrap chicken bones, apple cores, olive pits, and orange peels. It looked like a scene from *Tom Jones*. Their shotguns were still in the cases.

"Good to see you, Bob! Let me fix you a cold drink," Bill, said, working my hand like a bicycle pump.

"Thanks, Bill," I said.

He poured out a tall glass of iced tea.

"How about a chicken leg?" Margaret asked sweetly. She held out a plate of crispy fried drumsticks. "Bill and I will never eat all this," she whispered. "Take several. And have some deviled eggs."

Margaret was a fabulous cook. Furthermore, I hadn't had much lunch. Soon I was gobbling up whatever she offered, oblivious to everything around me.

The three of us were lost in a discussion about Cumberland lime pickles when I heard a shotgun go off. "Bang!" And then another. I came to my senses with a jolt. Guns were going off all over the field. Birds were flying. And they had been for some time.

"Good Lord! I've got to go!" I said.

"What's your hurry?" Margaret asked.

"The dove hunt ..."

"There's lots of time," she cooed seductively, holding out a plate of biscuits and country ham.

For a split second I hesitated, caught between two powerful desires. Then

I remembered that there's always a third option. I grabbed two or three biscuits, stuffed them in my pocket, and took off like a rabbit. As I hurried down the tractor road, I heard her calling out behind me, "Wait! You didn't get any stuffed celery!"

When I reached my stool, the hunt was in full swing. I could have kicked myself. I had blown valuable shooting time! Dropping a couple of field loads in my little side-by-side, I scanned the blue sky with renewed determination. I had to make up for lost time. The doves had started flying in on the west end. But that wasn't where the good gunners were positioned. Most of the old hands were set up on the east side. They sat watching patiently, waiting for their time to come.

I looked up and saw a pair of birds skimming the tree line. There was no way to know where they would turn into the field. My fingers tightened around the grip of my shotgun. But they cut in too soon. I watched the hunter stationed below them under the trees pivot 180 degrees as they cleared the canopy. He pulled on the first one going away. It fluttered to the ground like a torn kite. Then he smoked a second bird at about thirty-five yards out. Several people around him actually applauded. The man must have been someone's guest. No one at the club shot that well, including me. I sat there for a moment, looking on in admiration, imagining what it must have been like to take those two difficult birds in front of the whole gallery. Perhaps I could have done it once, but ...

"Bob! Oh, Bob!" Someone was waving a cigar in my face. It was the size of a cucumber.

"Oh, hi, Doc," I said.

"Here, take one of these," he insisted. "Let me light it for you."

"Maybe later. Listen I need to concentrate on ..."

"The Mrs. never lets me smoke these in the house," he continued. "Say, you've met my son, haven't you?"

"Yes, of course," I said, shaking hands with the young boy next to him.

"Damn it's good to be outdoors today, isn't it? Say, did I tell you about my trip to ..."

The story seemed to go on forever. Furthermore, he was standing between the field and me. I found myself peeking around his ear at the action. Shotguns were banging all over. Birds were flying. There was a damned dove shoot going on!

"Listen, Doc," I said, "I really need to ..."

"You know about guns, don't you?" he asked, blocking my escape.

"Well, some," I said impatiently.

"Look at my boy's 28. Do you think the stock's too short? Mount the gun, son, and show Mr. McDill."

His son obediently brought the little shotgun to his shoulder.

"Well, now is not a good ..."

"He's missed several birds in a row. The boy's gotten so much taller over the past year. I thought maybe ..."

Precious minutes were ticking by. I was getting desperate.

"I've got an idea," I said. "Why don't I let him shoot *my* gun?"

"Are you serious?"

"Sure. Looks like I'm not going to get to use it today."

He gave me an acrimonious look. "There's no need to be rude," he said. "I just thought someone with your experience might want to help."

"I'm sorry, Doc. But you see ..."

He turned abruptly and walked away muttering something to his son about how certain people take dove shooting much too seriously. I took a long pull on my water jug and told myself I'd make it up to them.

Four birds appeared over the middle of the field. They were low, cutting and turning over the bales and hides like broken field runners. Then they gained altitude, giving them a clear blue background. Now they were high enough for a safe shot. I felt an involuntary rush of energy, adrenaline. If they'd only turn my way!

"Hey, Bob!" someone shouted.

Whoever it is, I'll ignore him, I thought. The birds swept south toward the cornfield and over a group of teenage Lord Ripons. I glanced over to where the voice had come from. It was Roach Patton. He was sitting in the shade of a hackberry tree, leaning back in his dove chair. There was a smug smile on his face. Then I noticed a suspicious-looking glass in his hand.

"Gin and tonic?" he called out.

Hold it, I thought. *Roach knows better than that! After all these years as a member, and the man still has to be reminded of the rules!"* I walked over, my chest swelling with righteous indignation.

"Listen, Roach," I started in, "you know we don't allow drinking and shooting."

He let me go through the whole sermon. I covered safety, character, the sacred nature of birds on the wing, and the passing on of good practices to succeeding generations.

Then he grinned and said, "I know. But I'm through shooting."

"You're what?"

"I'm through. I limited out. Look, my gun's cased."

"But that can't be!"

"Yeah. I just shot my last bird a little while ago."

"What time is it anyway?" I asked, suddenly panicked.

"It's a quarter of five," he answered.

Where had the time gone? I got back in position as quickly as I could. By then, the birds were coming from the southeast corner. I watched them skim in over the treetops in threes and fours into the midst of several gunners hidden in a strip of uncut wheat. A high layer of cloud cover moved in, covering the sun. The temperature dropped a few degrees. I waited.

"Honey! Oh, Honey!" someone called to me.

"I won't answer," I thought.

"Oh, Sweetie!"

Since when did I get so freaking popular. If I had only had this kind of charisma in high school.

I saw her out of the corner of my eye, an elderly woman shouting and waving. She was old enough to be somebody's mother. Hell, she was old enough to be *my* mother. Sitting hidden behind a big hay bale at the edge of the field, she was wearing a khaki shirt buttoned up to her neck and a straw hat the size of a Yugo.

"Honey! Would you be a sweetheart and pick up that bird?" she asked.

"But I ..."

"It'll only take a minute," she pleaded.

"There's no way out of this," I thought. *If I refuse, I'll look like a character out of Charles Dickens.*

"Okay. Where did he fall?" I asked.

"Right near that tree. I'd come over there myself, but it's so hot, and I've been picking up birds all afternoon."

"Lucky you," I said under my breath. I hurried over to the place she had pointed out. "Right here you say?"

Glancing up, I saw three gray forms barreling down the west boundary of the field. There was one hide, a clump of tall weeds, between the pair and the edge. The man crouching behind it stood up. His first shot lagged the leader by a yard. But he was able to swing hard and drop the same bird with his second barrel. The remaining two cut back toward the tree line, sailing right over my stool, the place where I should have been sitting.

I kicked at the dead leaves and pushed grass aside with my foot. It's amazing how well camouflaged those little critters are. Against a background of hardwood leaves, they can be almost invisible. Suddenly, a shotgun went off near me, and a bird plunked into the deep brush behind me.

"Oh, Honey! Would you ...?"

"Of course! I've got nothing else to do," I mumbled.

All right. There's the first dove. Now to find the other one.

Crawling around in the bushes during snake season is one of my least favorite things. But I finally got both birds in hand and delivered them. The dear old lady thanked me sweetly. Then she forced me to drink a glass of lemonade.

"There were so many more doves when my husband, Chester, was alive," she said sadly.

"Yes, ma'am," I answered.

As soon as I could get away, I started toward my stool at a trot. I could still get in a few minutes. But to my surprise, I met Deacon Maxwell coming toward me carrying all his gear.

"Deacon, where are you going?"

"I'm afraid it's about time to close our hymnbooks and take up the collection," he said smiling, proud of the metaphor.

"You mean you're leaving the field?"

"Well, they've just about quit flying. After all, it *is* six o'clock."

"What?"

"It's six o'clock," he repeated. "I'm afraid it's all over, old friend."

"Noooooooooooooooo!"

That evening, the front yard of the old clubhouse looked like an outdoor cafe in some French village. Paper lanterns were strung in the trees. Decorations made of cornstalks and sunflowers dotted the tabletops. Some people had changed out of their sweaty shooting clothes and stood around looking fresh and rested. Slick Lawson had switched into his role as executive chef. He was stationed behind the serving table in a tall white chef's hat, ladling out dove breasts with Madeira sauce, wild rice, corn on the cob, and garden tomatoes with chopped basil. I waited at the edge of the lawn with a couple of friends. We were killing a few minutes until the serving line went down.

"That was some shoot today, wasn't it?" one of my friends said.

"It was one of the best we've ever had," the other exclaimed. "They say we bagged over 200 birds."

"So, how did you do anyway?" the first asked the second.

"Well, it's unusual for me," he said modestly, "but I shot pretty well. I got just short of a limit. What about you?"

"Considering the chances I had, I should have limited out," he said, not to be outdone in the modesty department. "As it was, I got ten."

Then, the question I knew was coming came. One of them turned to me and asked, "How about you, Bob? How many did you bag?"

They both looked on expectantly, waiting for a response. But it was okay. I'd thought it over, and I had my answer.

"Well, I'll tell you the truth, fellows," I said. "It really doesn't matter. To me, a dove hunt's more of a social occasion."

2

The Messenger

From *Shooting Sportsman*

Eleven months out of the year, the Deacon was a sane man. In fact more than sane, he was absolutely stalwart. The nickname "Deacon" was well deserved since he was an elected deacon in the First Presbyterian Church and rarely missed a Sunday service. He was also a devoted husband and family man and could be seen at every ball game, play, and recital in which his children participated. In business, his reputation was stellar. He handled his clients' money with the utmost probity and was trusted to arrange their estates so that, in the event of some tragedy, the orphaned descendants would

ISTOCK

be fed, clothed, and educated in the bosom of some giant insurance company. He was a man you could depend on, the kind you could turn to. Yes, for eleven months out of a year Mr. M. Porter Maxwell, or the Deacon, was a pillar, a rock, a brick. It was during that twelfth month that he went off the skids.

It was a Friday afternoon. I stood staring out my office window at the latest installment of snow. It was coming down intermittently in big clumps as if someone were plucking a goose on the roof of our building. The temperature had been stuck below freezing for a week. This was weather that made waterfowl leave the confines of the refuge and go in search of food and open water, in other words, active. If I left now, I could be at the duck camp by two. Then the receptionist buzzed me.

"Yes?"

"It's Mrs. Maxwell," she informed me.

"Yes, of course, I'll take it. Hello, Marie. How are you?"

"I'm fine, Bob," came the sweet voice on the other end. "And you?"

"I'm fine." I waited for her to get down to businesses. Marie was not in the habit of calling me to chat.

"I was just wondering if you might be going to the duck camp?"

"Yes, as a matter of fact I am."

"Good. Could I trouble you to give my husband a message?"

"It's no trouble."

"Please tell him that several of his clients have been calling his office. Some of them are getting a little ... impatient."

"Yes, of course."

"And tell him that his son's coach has been calling. It's something about a basketball scholarship, and he insists on talking to both parents."

"Okay," I said. "I'll give him the message."

"And also the pipes in his Aunt Ruthy's house are frozen. She's quite old and doesn't know who else to ..."

"Okay." By now I'd made use of my notepad. "Anything else?"

"Well, only that my car won't start. I guess the battery's frozen or something."

All this was related without the slightest hint of anger or frustration. This was a woman of strength and self-reliance, a woman raised and hardened in a waterfowling family. She had learned as a child to accept certain behavior among men during duck season as normal. In that way Deacon was a lucky man.

The drive to the duck camp took an extra hour. A new layer of snow had slowed traffic on the interstate to a cautious thirty-five. When I turned onto Cuba Landing Road, I noticed that there were no new tire tracks. No one had been in or out since the last dusting. As I pulled up to the lodge I saw the Deacon's green Jeep parked in its usual place. Actually the lodge was an ancient farmhouse leaning noticeably to starboard, but calling it a lodge gave the place a certain dignity. Judging from the snow halfway up the wheels, the Jeep hadn't been moved in days. I suddenly felt uneasy. Perhaps he'd run into trouble or worse. Perhaps I was about to come upon the scene of some tragedy. Then I saw a thin column of smoke rising from the bunkroom chimney. Behind the house was a well-trod trail from the back door to the creek.

When I entered the front hallway, I was unprepared for what I saw. There were dead ducks hanging from every nail, peg, and doorknob. Mallards, widgeons, gadwalls, and teal, they hung strapped together like clusters of ripe grapes, the fruit of some Old Testament harvest. I opened the bunkroom door.

"Deacon!" I called out. "Deacon! You here?"

Then I saw him. He was huddled next to the wood stove with a blanket around him. Only the top of his head was visible. I'd almost overlooked him in the confusion of clothing and gear strewn around the room.

"Are you all right?" I asked.

He lowered the blanket and peered at me. I couldn't help noticing a four- or five-day growth of beard. There was soot smeared on his face, evidence of tending that day's fire. All this gave his eyeballs a startling whiteness.

"Of course I'm all right," he answered. "Why wouldn't I be? Come in! Come in!"

The Deacon's old Lab, Bo, lay at his feet. In an effort to get as much of his body under the warm stove as possible, he had flattened himself out to such an extent that, for a moment, I mistook him for a rug.

"Ranger Bob, I'm glad you're here!" the Deacon shouted.

Most of the club members called me Ranger Bob. I got the name because I once insisted on pouring a bucket of water on a campfire, even though everyone else contended it was already out. At a duck camp, a little thing like that can stick to a man for a lifetime.

"Listen, Ranger. Did you bring any ammo?"

"Yes, plenty."

"Good! Let me tell you about the ..."

"Excuse me, Deacon. But how long have you been here?"

"Oh, about a week I think."

"Maybe you should've called home or something."

"Couldn't. Cell phone's dead," he said cheerfully.

"But there's a phone at the store up on the ..."

"Jeep's frozen up," he replied with a grin. He waved his hand to dismiss my badgering. "Now, let me tell you about the hunting."

"Yes, sure. Just let me put my gear away."

I tossed my sleeping bag onto my favorite bunk and walked into the kitchen. The room was so cold, my breath was visible. Obviously the power was out.

"Don't use the bathroom!" the Deacon shouted. "The pipes are frozen."

When I opened the refrigerator door to put away the groceries I'd brought, all I found inside was an ancient box of baking soda and half a can of Mountain Dew. The pantry was just as empty.

"What did you have for dinner last night?" I called out.

"Grilled duck," he answered.

"What about lunch?"

"Leftover duck."

"Breakfast?"

"Duck and eggs."

"That sounds good," I said, trying to put a positive spin on things.

"But I was out of eggs."

I returned to the bunkroom, closing the door tightly behind me to preserve the heat.

"Sit down," the Deacon said. "Wait until you hear about the duck hunting."

I took a seat by the fire. As the Deacon began to talk excitedly, I noticed that the sleeves of his long underwear, which extended an inch or so past the cuffs of his mackinaw shirt, were ringed with soot.

"When Bo and I got here," he began, "I figured things were about to break open. It was last uh ... well, whatever day it was. Anyway, this cold front had just moved in, and I knew it was time for the big flocks to come off the refuge and move into the bottoms looking for food. And I was right. When we topped the levee that first morning, I could hear them. All those fat mallards out there chomping on those ears of corn, all those plump little widgeons munching up those grass seeds, and all those gadwalls eating ... well, eating whatever it is gadwalls eat. When we slipped into old No.7, they started taking to the air around us by the hundreds. But we were as quiet as a couple of potted plants. We sat there and didn't fire a shot. Because I knew, as sure as John Wayne was a Republican, in about thirty minutes they'd start coming back in groups of six to a dozen. So I held back, Ranger! I held back."

"That's good, Deacon."

"In a half hour, the first bunch reappeared. All mallards. A new snow had started up, and they came out of it with their wings already cupped. Then I saw that there were more birds higher up! Then I looked above those and saw another group above that!"

His voice was rising now with excitement.

"They were in layers, Ranger, layers! And all of them determined to light right in our deeks! So there we were, just Bo and me, in the midst of the most glorious morning of duck hunting since Nash Buckingham! Just the two of us, while our entire sissy club membership, uh ... present company excluded of course, while our entire sissy club membership was back in the city watching some silly ball game on TV. And they've been flying every morning since, just like that."

"That's great, Deacon. Listen, Marie asked me to tell you ... Well, maybe it would be best if you called her. And you might check in with your office too."

I handed him my cell phone. He took it from me and looked at it curiously, turning it over in his hand, as if it were some gadget from another world.

"Oh, yes. Check in. Yes, of course."

He sat for a minute longer as if coming to himself. Then he took the phone, slipped on his coat, and walked out the front door. I watched him pass the bunkroom window. He was on his way to a spot behind the lodge that had proven best for cell phone reception. After a half hour or so, he came back inside and slumped into his chair by the wood stove.

"You check in?" I asked.

"Oh, yes," he answered. "It seems a couple of clients have been calling my office every hour for the last couple of days. Every hour! For some people, the sky is always falling. I'll have to hold their hands till things right themselves."

He stared into the fire a long time without speaking.

"And Aunt Ruthy's pipes are frozen, poor thing," he said finally. "I need to take care of that."

He took the poker and pushed an errant piece of wood to the back of the stove.

"My son's basketball coach wants a conference. He's been trying to get in touch. And Marie's car won't start. She can't get to the grocery."

The sparkle in his eyes was gone now. The gleeful man who'd sat there a half hour ago had been transformed into a spiritless lump. He was now a middle-aged businessman, a father, and a husband faced with duty, responsibility.

Then he turned and looked at me. At first I thought he was peering past me at some object on the wall. But no, he was staring directly at me. He simply wasn't seeing me. His eyes had become opaque, impenetrable, as if they were seeing not what was in front of them, but something else that only the Deacon could see. Then a smile began, ever so meagerly at the corners of his mouth. It spread in small increments until it covered his whole face.

"But you know what, Ranger Bob?"

"What, Deacon?"

"All that stuff can wait," he said. "Because I think they're going to fly again in the morning."

3

The Captain and the Reelfoot Stove

From *Shooting Sportsman*

I suppose it all had to come to a head. At some point, it was inevitable that things would reach some sort of climax. Ill feeling had been building up at the Old River Rod and Gun, Bloody Mary Society and Gentlemen's Club all season. For the first time in anyone's memory, mumbled curses were heard around the lodge after the morning duck hunt. And on several evenings, arguments had even broken out at the dinner table. The hostility was directed at our own Captain Anderson.

Ordinarily the Captain was a favorite among the members. As a retired naval officer and engineer, he was usually a handy fellow to have around. No one was as clever with mechanical things as the Captain. For example, he was quite an asset when somebody's shotgun went on the fritz.

"Captain, my old A5 was shucking them awful slow this morning," somebody might say.

"Hand her over!" the Captain would order. Then he'd retire to his work area, an oily spot at the end of the kitchen table. After a half hour of grunting and cursing, he'd return the shotgun to its owner along with a scolding, "Hell, man, you had your selenium dido positioned behind your gobbler switch!"

"I did? Oh, sorry, Cap."

The Captain was an inventor too. And most of his inventions had been pretty successful. The automatic decoy washer was a big hit. And his wind-powered game feeder worked pretty well as long as a good wind was blowing.

The trouble began when the Captain spent a weekend hunting ducks at Reelfoot Lake. His guide there introduced him to a gadget called the Reelfoot Stove. The Reelfoot Stove was a simple little contraption designed to warm a duck blind. It was no more than a steel box sitting on four legs with a chimney at one end. The top was on hinges so that charcoal could be put inside. There were a dozen ports and vents around the sides, which, I believe, the Captain liked best of all since they required lots of tinkering and adjusting. Anyway, he was so impressed with the little contraption he took the idea home to his workshop and built his own version, which he claimed was much improved over the original.

The morning things finally reached a crisis was an unusually mild one for January. The water around the duck blinds had thawed, and there was a thick mist rising in the cornstalks. The Captain and Pogo Walters were in the willow blind, a little two-man outfit near the river. Pinky Lipman, Walter Matthau, and I had drawn old No. 7. No, I don't mean Walter Matthau, the movie actor. This man's name was Melvin Creamclot. But he looked a lot like Walter Matthau so that's what we called him. He was a tall, stoop-shouldered man with droopy jowls.

"Things have warmed up a little," Walter Matthau announced.

"Yes, they have," Pinky agreed.

"But mark my words, the Captain will soon be firing up that infernal stove of his."

"Oh, no doubt about that," Pinky replied.

"Well, it's Pogo's problem this morning," Walter Matthau said.

Duck hunting at the Old River had never been what you might call spectacular. Oh, we had a good year now and then. But the difficulty had always been in putting two good seasons together back to back. It seemed that if the birds liked our river bottom one year, they usually liked someplace else better the next. There were great shoots written down in the old club logs, but time seemed to put more and more distance between those glory days and the present. Still, the old farmhouse that we self-importantly called "the lodge" was accommodating. And we owned a good stretch of frontage on the river, which was our ticket to the smallmouth spawn in the spring. And even if the duck season was dismal, men get comfortable in their surroundings. They are reluctant to leave old friends and places behind. So the membership remained mostly unchanged.

The best time to shoot a duck at the Old River had always been at sunrise. There, in that hour of half light, before the sun fully lit the bare trees and illuminated the fields, the ducks, if there were any, lifted onto the air and hesitated, not sure if they wanted to leave for the safety of the big lake on the refuge or remain in our bottom to feed on the ample corn, milo, and native grasses. With sharp eyes, stillness, and careful calling, a bird or two might be brought to hand.

Unfortunately sunrise was precisely the time the Captain had been starting up the Reelfoot Stove. He usually began by filling the little box to the brim with charcoal. Next, he stuffed in a couple of issues of the *Wall Street Journal*. He was not a man to be stingy with material. More was always better with the Captain. Finally, all this was drenched with a gallon or so of diesel fuel. Then the whole business was touched off with a big wooden kitchen match.

When the initial roar of the diesel fuel subsided, he began what he called "fine tuning," that is adjusting the little ports and vents on the sides of the box. First he'd open one, then another, then regulate a third to perhaps half open, enjoying himself immensely. But no matter what adjustments he made, great clouds of smoke soon boiled out of the stove. It was as if the little box were connected to the gates of hell. The blinding smoke sent most hunters out the back door of the blind for air. Pogo Walters once fired into the billows claiming he'd seen a "fire duck." It later turned out to be a flaming airborne page from the *Wall Street Journal*.

"Shhh," Pinky whispered to Walter Matthau and me, interrupting my thoughts.

"Why?" I asked.

"Not so loud," he said. "I can hear the Captain and Pogo talking. So they might be able to hear us."

"The Captain already knows my opinion on that stink box of his!" Walter Matthau volunteered in an overly loud voice. "If he hears it one more time, it won't bother me!"

Pinky was right. We could hear voices from the willow blind with perfect clarity. Over Pogo's fervent protests, the Captain was about to fire up the Reelfoot Stove.

"Oh, gee, Cap, why do you have to light that blasted thing?"

"To take the chill off, Po. A little warmth will be nice."

"But I'm not cold."

"You'll be cold later. It hasn't set in yet. Anyway, there's nothing like a toasty warm duck blind."

"Even if I were cold, which I'm not," Pogo countered, "I'd rather be cold than put up with that stinking, smoking contraption of yours."

"I've never seen people make such an issue out of a little smoke."

"A little smoke, hell! Anyway, what's that you're pouring on top?"

"It's something I made up last night. Your complaint about the smoke has been duly noted and duly remedied. So why don't you just sit back and enjoy a nice warm hunt?"

"But why are you pouring on so much?"

"I suggest you leave the engineering to me, and I'll leave the car selling to you," the Captain replied.

"Auto leasing," Pogo corrected him.

"Whatever."

"Good Lord, you're going to kill us," Pogo said.

"Nonsense."

Next, three events occurred in rapid succession. First, there was a flash of light. Not what you'd call a blinding flash but sufficient to illuminate the surrounding landscape and make each cornstalk stand out in graphic relief. Second, a sound came from the willow blind, which might best be described as a "vooom" or a "whoosh." Third, a black mushroom cloud appeared above it. It was an exact duplicate, in miniature, of the mushroom clouds seen over atomic test sites in Arizona. After that succession of events, chaos ensued. A flame appeared in the dry cornstalks on top of the blind and engulfed the little structure in a matter of seconds.

"Aaaaaaggghhhhhhhh!" Pogo wailed.

"Out the back!" the Captain shouted.

"Where's the door?" Pogo bellowed. "I can't see!"

In a split second, the Captain crashed through the back door of the blind and lay sprawling in the mud.

"I'm going to diiiiiieee!" Pogo howled from inside.

But he didn't die. A moment later, he came over the top, through the flames, like some circus animal jumping through a fiery hoop. His momentum was such that he landed in the decoy spread, a good fifteen feet out. When he hit the shallow water, he made a hissing sound like a hot piece of iron. For several seconds Pogo lay still. Then he slowly got to his feet. The Captain stood a good distance away from the inferno that was now the willow blind as he brushed the mud from his coat and trousers. Then Pogo saw him.

"I'm going to kill yoooouuuuu!" he bellowed.

Pogo started forward through the shallow water, his arms extended in front of him like an old-time zombie in a horror movie. A half-dozen mallard decoys, tangled in his hip waders, trailed behind him.

"And then, do you know what I'm going to do with that Reelfoot Stove?" he shouted.

The Captain was surprisingly quick for an older man. He picked up his old Remington and headed for the tree line, not quite running but at a fast walk. It appeared for a moment that Pogo would cut him off. But seeing he was beaten, Pogo turned and made for the nearest shore. By the time he reached landfall, the Captain had disappeared.

After that weekend, Pogo's temper cooled. By nature, he was not a violent man. Still, he refused to see the Captain for the balance of the season. If the Captain was expected at the club, Pogo made a point of not being there.

"He's making a big deal out of it," the Captain said. "I've been hurt worse than that grilling hamburgers."

Pogo wasn't seriously burned. He might have had his hair singed off if it had not been for his old corduroy hunting cap that had been pulled down over his ears. As it was, he'd only lost his eyebrows. Without eyebrows to mark where his forehead began, his face looked unusually long, rather like a horse or a mule. It would've been better if Pogo had left things as they were. People could have grown used to his equine appearance. And eventually, his eyebrows would have grown back. But for whatever reason, his wife decided to draw on a new set. And instead of putting them back as they had been, she painted on a pair much like her own, two high sweeping arcs. This gave Pogo a startled look. Someone suggested he looked like a member of the cast of *Gypsy*.

Duck season ended, summer passed, and autumn came again at the Old River. With a fall chill in the air there was, once again, a hardwood fire in the parlor fireplace. Another waterfowl season was approaching. And as always, the members talked about it hopefully, sure that this one would rival the old days. Fresh cane and oak brush were added to the duck blinds. The dog stands and ladders were repaired, and the floors of the blinds were shored up. And finally, stops were put in the water structures, and the water began rising week after week, flooding the corn and native grasses along the river.

It was at about that time that those little propane-fueled heaters appeared in all the sporting goods stores. After much pressure from the members and Pogo actually threatening to put his membership up for sale, our president, Deacon Maxwell, went out and bought one, with club funds of course. It proved to be a marvelous little device. Not only did it create a large amount of heat, it was odorless and smokeless. But the Captain never took to it. I suspect part of the reason was its simplicity. It had only one knob. That single knob controlled all functions. He finally refused to touch it, declaring that its operation was not deserving of his expertise.

4

The Beleaguered Bunny

From *Shooting Sportsman*

I owed Billy a favor. In fact, I owed him several favors. It seemed that every time I needed him, I'd hear a knock on the door, and he'd be standing there with a beer in his hand and a willing grin on his face. He lived only a mile up the road from the Old River Rod and Gun, Bloody Mary Society and Gentlemen's Club. He was an electrician by trade, but he also knew carpentry and plumbing.

That particular Saturday as I was struggling to put electric heat in the TV room of the lodge, Billy dropped by again. He wired the heater into the breaker box and checked the amperage. Then he assured me I was not about to burn down one of the oldest structures in Humphreys County. I was in Billy's debt, no doubt about it, so when he asked if he could take some friends rabbit hunting on the property the next day, I quickly said yes. But then he invited me along. I mumbled a string of excuses. But it was Billy asking, so I finally agreed to join them.

I'm not really a rabbit hunter. I hadn't shot a rabbit since I was a boy when the occasional dumb cottontail would poke his head up out of the briars and I'd knock him over with my .410. Furthermore, I've spent most of my adult life in the company of waterfowlers and bird hunters. Some of them have a certain disdain, snootiness even, about hunting critters. "I don't shoot fur," a friend of mine once remarked.

I personally don't like shotgun snobs and don't consider myself to be one. But I didn't consider rabbit hunting to be great sport, so I was less than enthusiastic. There may be a certain incongruity in this American attitude, however. I once saw a film of the British royal family shooting at Balmoral. There they were, dressed in estate tweeds, banging away at rabbits. I looked closely to see if their royal noses were in the air. They were not. I ascertained from this that they didn't consider themselves to be slumming. And I know firsthand that gamekeepers on British estates have no prejudice against the rabbit. If one comes racing out of the heather, a shooter is expected to bag it. It goes in the day's count along with the grouse or pheasant. Restaurants in London certainly have nothing against it. With all this in mind, I revised my options. Duck season was over. The snipe had moved on. Perhaps I'd go along for the exercise.

Sunday morning arrived bright and cold, but Billy had told me earlier that we'd need to wait until the frost melted off the grass. "Frost obscures the scent," he said. At nine o'clock, he and his brother Chris arrived. As we stood on the front porch of the lodge exchanging greetings, an aging pickup truck pulled into the front yard behind my Jeep. It had a big wooden box in the bed, which, judging by its pitched roof, might have been a child's playhouse. But I knew it had to be a dog kennel. A slight silver-haired man climbed out. This was Harry Gatlin, master of beagle hounds, and as I later found out, a somewhat famous local character. He had on brand-new jeans and a red mackinaw

ISTOCK

shirt. In the crook of his arm, he carried an ancient pump that didn't have a hint of blueing on it. He smiled and graciously thanked me for the hunt. I thanked him for bringing his dogs.

Anxious to get started, Billy and Chris were already transferring ammo from an open box into their hunting jackets. I picked up my little 20 gauge bird gun. Billy had suggested I bring along some lead no. 6s. No problem, pheasant loads. Harry went back to the truck and opened the kennel door. Seven dogs tumbled out, each one the exact same size and bearing almost identical markings. Two pups were in the group, and Harry informed me that if we had a good day, they'd learn something.

We followed Billy and Chris, who were about to disappear around the corner of the lodge. Harry called to the dogs, and they puttered along behind us. When we reached the edge of the backyard, Harry stopped and looked down at the dogs expectantly. They began to nose their way into the thicket. Then they went to work, first up the east levee along the lake, where the briars are thick and knee high. Chris climbed over the fence and took up duties in Rochelle's pasture on the right. The rest of us walked the open levee on the left. After a few minutes, one of the older dogs let out a howl. Billy and Chris couldn't contain themselves. They let out a few yelps and howls of their own. Harry wasn't surprised at this. He grinned at me and said, "Okay, here we go." The other dogs joined the one that had struck the scent. They fell in line behind her, and the race was on. There then rose a chorus of yowls and yips that would stir the soul of even the most hardened bird hunter. Down the levee they went, loping along at a trot where the cover would allow, then crawling where it was thick. I heard a splash in the creek on the right side of the levee. By then, the dogs had turned and started back in our direction.

"There he goes," Chris shouted as the rabbit escaped across Rochelle's pasture and out of shotgun range. The dogs trailed up to the creek and grew quiet. They sniffed at the edge of the water where the trail ended. But no matter how well developed their noses, nothing in their intelligence suggested they cross the water. Whether it was luck or wit, the first bunny had eluded us.

The dogs scattered in all directions, intent on new sport. Soon, one of them struck a fresh scent, and the cacophony went up again. After a short chase, the rabbit came bounding out of the thicket. This one was on open ground and in range of Harry's shotgun. Harry rolled him into a furry heap. A few minutes later Chris bagged one. Then Billy. They had four bunnies by the time we reached the end of the levee. It had taken less than an hour. But I had yet to pull the trigger. Perhaps I was still feeling a little smug. And after all, I was—or so I'd told myself—just along for the exercise. Whatever my thinking was, it was about to change.

We reached the end of the levee and started down the bank. The dogs struck a new scent on a patch of cane and headed into the bottom. I saw the rabbit race across open ground and into a stand of corn. This field had been flooded for ducks only a few weeks earlier, but now it was so dry I could hear the stalks rattling in the breeze. We spread out. I moved a short distance down the field to what seemed like a likely place for the rabbit to exit. The breeze had suddenly died down. But at a distance of about fifty yards, I could see the cornstalks flutter as the dogs moved through them. They were really bellowing and howling now in what Harry called "full voice." The sound was chilling, wonderful, and ancient. Just then there was a movement at the edge of the corn. Out he came, full throttle, I swung on, and he tumbled. I was about to go over and pick him up when I heard Harry's voice behind me. "If you don't mind, Bob, let him lay," he said. The dogs soon broke into the open. Harry picked up the rabbit as they gathered round. "We'll let them get a good smell," he said. "They'll know this one's dead, and they won't follow his scent anymore."

I was astonished. "You mean they can tell one rabbit's scent from another?" I asked.

"Amazing, ain't it?" Harry answered.

The sun was warming things up by then, so we hung our coats on fence posts to be retrieved later. By late morning we'd circled the front side of the farm and bagged another rabbit or two. Harry said the dogs were tired. They were getting sloppy. So we decided to take a lunch break and hunt the rest of the property in the afternoon. The big circle we'd made that morning had brought us back to the lodge. Harry put the dogs in the kennel so they could rest, and we laid the rabbits out in a line on the front porch. We had eight, and Harry pronounced them all fat and healthy. He pointed out the younger ones and declared that they'd be the most tender. Chris had driven to the store up on the highway for sandwiches and cold drinks. While we ate, we complimented each other on our shooting and the dogs on how well they had performed. Harry was pleased.

That afternoon we hunted the back side of the property. I noticed Harry carrying a pint of Jack Daniel's in his pants pocket. He caught my eye and asked if I objected. I didn't. He unloaded his gun and said he didn't plan to shoot anymore. He only wanted to work the dogs. The Jack Daniel's and the warm afternoon sun soon lifted his spirits. He became talkative. It was all about rabbit dogs: buying, selling, trading, who was good to his dogs, who wasn't, big beagles versus little beagles. I even learned that Harry had been offered $300 for Dixie and a brand-new Remington auto for Belle. Just as we rounded a patch of woods along the back fence, one of the dogs yelped. A bunny shot through the brush about forty yards out. I heard two shotguns report, but this rabbit was really flying. Without thinking, I swung hard and pulled the trigger as the front bead passed his nose. Then I followed through with the swing. He tumbled. Compliments were shouted from all directions. I was, of course, very pleased. A fast target at forty yards, partially obscured by cover, is not a given. Then I remembered the sporting clays course and the Fur and Feather stand. I'd practiced this event dozens of times. This was one bunny shot I knew something about. I returned an off-handed "thank you," but didn't give away my secret. Then Harry told us about the group he'd hunted with the previous week.

"They couldn't hit a thing," he said. "The dogs ran the same two or three rabbits all afternoon." This made Billy and Chris and me feel pretty good about ourselves.

When we reached the back corner of the farm, we propped our shotguns against some saplings and sat down in the grass. We were thirsty, and our feet hurt. The rabbits were heavy. I told them that when in the Scottish Highlands, two pony boys lead a pony a good distance behind the hunting party. The pony carries sandwiches, beer, and all the bagged game. Harry, Billy, and Chris decided this was a fine practice. They resolved to hire someone for that very purpose next year. This was the first I'd heard about "next year," but I realized I was all for it. It had been a wonderful day and great sport. As for any future defense of what now appears to be my annual rabbit hunt, I'm ready. If some tweedy, anglophile upland bird snob says anything snooty, I know how I'll respond. "You mean rabbit shooting isn't considered great sport here in the States?" I'll ask with just a hint of an English accent. "Why in Britain, even the royal family ..."

5

The Care and Treatment of Camp Cooks

From *A Guitar and a Pen*

A moment before, Spoony Odom had stood up from his place at the kitchen table and started toward the door. Dinner was over, and the only duties left were washing the dishes and utensils, something Spoony never participated in. At the door he paused to untie his apron as if he had forgotten it until just that moment. Then Beagle noticed him standing there, looking back at the men seated at the long kitchen table, waiting for recognition.

"Magnificent dinner, Spoony!" Beagle called out.

"Oh, thank you," the camp cook said, his face flushing.

"Yes, that one was over the top!" Beagle continued.

"Oh, you don't mean that," Spoony said.

"Those New Orleans chefs can take a backseat to you, my friend," Deacon Maxwell added. He pushed his chair back from the table and folded his hands across his ample stomach.

"You're all too kind," Spoony said, fumbling with his apron strings.

He was a small man, perhaps a size or two smaller than the other club members, with fine silver-gray hair, which he kept carefully combed. His facial features were well proportioned and almost delicate.

"By golly, you should open a restaurant!" The Deacon declared. The Deacon was often the first one to sit down for dinner and the last one to leave.

"Oh, go on," Spoony returned, turning a little red.

"No. I'm serious. You'd have people lined up around the block!" The Deacon had begun scraping the last of the chocolate mousse out of a pot on top of the stove.

Finally, when every compliment that could be thought of had been delivered, Spoony turned and left the kitchen. While the club members washed dishes, he sat alone by the fire in the TV room, sipping a tiny cup of espresso.

The Old River Rod and Gun, Bloody Mary Society and Gentlemen's Club wasn't the largest hunting camp around, nor did it offer the best shooting and fishing. But it had something no other club had. It had Spoony Odom. Among camp cooks, he was a legend. Spoony was no chili and beer man. Not by a long shot. He followed the New Orleans and European styles in culinary matters. He was a maker of sauces and stocks, a sauteer. He had a flair for presentation. And he was a genius with desserts. Spoony was not a hired chef. With the stingy dues we paid at the Old River, we could never have afforded such a thing. He was a club member and cooked simply for the love of it, and of course, for the adulation he received.

His menus were based on what was fresh and seasonal. Waterfowl were favored during the winter months, and quail and dove (if enough could be collected) in autumn. In summer, he specialized in the fish that were plentiful in our reservoir. A camp favorite was pan-seared bass with maître dhôtel sauce. Simple side dishes of rice pilaf and sliced tomatoes with fresh basil usually accompanied it. He often paired this treat with a crisp chilled Chardonnay.

There are three rules concerning the care and treatment of camp cooks. Rule 1: No matter what the cook does or says, he's treated with groveling courtesy. Rule 2: The cook is never asked to perform any task other than cooking. Rule 3: The cook's food is never, ever criticized. We followed the first rule to the letter at the Old River. As for the second, we had no choice in the matter. Spoony knew his rights. If anyone had suggested he help wash dishes, he would have been incensed. And as for painting or carpentry, it was out of the question.

But I did see the third rule violated once. Dawn had broken clear and cold over the marsh that Saturday morning. Duck hunting had been good that season, and old blind No. 7 was filled with hunters. The night before, Spoony had put together a culinary masterpiece. It had begun with leek soup. The next course was grilled mallard breast with plum sauce, served with porcini mushroom risotto, and wild mustard greens. This was accompanied by a hardy Beaujolais. Dessert was New Orleans bread pudding. Obviously, Spoony felt he hadn't had enough praise the night before.

"How was the dinner last night, fellows?" he asked innocently.

Beagle decided to take the ball. He was a lawyer. If anybody could lay it on, it was Beagle.

"A magnificent repast, my friend!" he said.

"But what did you *really* think?" Spoony queried.

"A culinary masterpiece!" Beagle added.

"Really? Was it as good as usual?"

"Each one is more magnificent than the last," Beagle said, summing up.

"Well, I really want to know if there was anything amiss," Spoony said, dragging out the discussion.

You do?" Pinky Lipman asked. Pinky removed his porkpie hat and pushed back a shock of hair as if gathering his thoughts.

"Of course," Spoony said.

"Well ..." Pinky stammered.

"What is it?" Spoony asked.

"The soup was, was ... a little salty," Pinky squeaked.

A collective gasp arose from everyone present.

"What?" Spoony asked, not sure he had heard correctly.

"The soup might have been a little salty," Pinky repeated.

There was a second gasp.

"Oh, boy. Now you've done it," the Deacon whispered from the back of the blind.

And he had. Spoony turned as cold and silent as the South Pole. For the rest of the morning, he looked off at the horizon as if he were searching the sky for ducks. When spoken to, he was curt and sullen. After reconsidering, Pinky apologized, saying he'd been wrong about the soup.

"No, no," Spoony snapped back. "I'm sure you're right. I suppose it was terrible."

By cocktail hour his mood hadn't changed. At seven he was sitting alone in the TV room and had made no move to start dinner. If it hadn't been for the hundreds of new ducks that had poured into our fields that afternoon on the heels of a cold front, he might have left the club in a huff.

The rest of us huddled in the kitchen.

"Well, what was I supposed to say?" Pinky said, defending himself.

"You know how Spoony is," the Deacon scolded. "Why did you have to open your big pudding hole?"

"Well, he asked us, didn't he?" Pinky whined. "He wanted to know if anything was wrong."

"Since when did you become a soup expert anyway?" the Deacon continued. "When you joined this club, you didn't know what a leek was."

Finally the group came to a decision. They decided that I was to be their spokesman.

"You're his friend," the Deacon pleaded. "You can talk to him."

I was not aware that I was Spoony's friend, that is, any more or less than the other members. After all, Spoony was a difficult man. But off I went, representing the whole membership, knowing a lifetime of canned chili and saltines might lie ahead of us. When I entered the TV room, he was sitting in his favorite chair and staring at the fire.

"Evening, Spoon," I said as cheerfully as possible.

"Evening," he said sullenly.

"It's getting on toward dinnertime, Spoon," I hinted.

"Oh, I won't be cooking tonight," he answered.

"Why not, Spoon? If it's Pinky, I can ..."

"Oh no," he interrupted, "just don't feel up to it, you see."

I passed the bad news on to the others. That night each of us made himself a cold sandwich. The big table in the kitchen looked strangely bare with only cheese, sandwich meat, and a few other things dotting its long surface. Spoony's chair, normally the one closest to the stove, was conspicuously empty. Only the week before he had prepared his goose and sausage gumbo. The smell and taste of it were still fresh in my memory. The roux had been rich and dark, the sausage spicy, and the goose succulent. There was a salad of baby greens and fresh watercress. Two loaves of hot French bread had been passed around the table.

It was an above average year for duck hunting. Spoony continued to show up at the club every weekend, but he went nowhere near the kitchen. He cleaned his birds carefully as always and put them in the freezer. The Deacon claimed that he had seen him eating a turkey on brown bread sandwich in his car. Beagle tried to appeal to his vanity, "A man of your great talent, my friend, has a duty to his companions and to his club, indeed to the world!"

But Spoony claimed that he had lost interest in cooking. He went on to say that thirty years devoted to the pursuit and perfection of a single art were probably enough. Furthermore he was now considering taking up the five-string banjo. Some members actually began staying home with their families on weekends. Finally Beagle came up with a plan. It was a long shot, but it was all we had. We cornered Pinky and laid out the details.

"I'm just not comfortable with this," he said, protesting.

"Why not?" Beagle asked.

"Well, for one thing, it's not honest."

"I wouldn't quite call it dishonest," Beagle said.

"But I'd be telling a lie."

"I wouldn't quite call it a lie," Beagle added.

"Look, I won't say Spoony and I are close or anything, but it just wouldn't be right, making up this cockamamie story and all."

"Think of the members," the Deacon pleaded.

"No. I really don't think I can do it," Pinky said.

"Look," the Deacon demanded, "you can fish, can't you?"

"Yes."

"Then you can lie."

"Okay, okay," Pinky said, holding up his hands in surrender.

He found the camp cook in the kitchen, ceremoniously packing his spices into a cardboard box.

"Spoon?" he began carefully.

"Yes?" Spoony answered.

"There's something you ought to know," Pinky said. "Tonight I was telling some of the fellows and, well, you see ..."

"What is it?" Spoony asked impatiently

"I've sort of run into a rough patch," he said.

Spoony stared at the label on a bottle of coriander and said coolly, "Oh? What kind of rough patch?"

"It's my health, Spoon."

"It's your heart, isn't it?" Spoony responded. "I've told you before, all you fellows eat too much fat."

"No, no, it's not my heart," Pinky said, pausing for effect. "I've been hiding this from you and the other members. But I can't hide it any longer. It's my brain."

"Your brain?" Spoony asked, looking up.

"Yes, you see I've been diagnosed with a ... disorder." He looked at Spoony carefully, trying to judge his reaction.

Spoony was caught off guard. "Disorder?" he asked.

"Yes."

"Well, hhhow bad is it?" Spoony stammered.

"I'm afraid it's pretty bad. Soon I'll surrender most of my mental faculties," Pinky said, as if reading from a textbook.

Oh," Spoony said, his eyes growing wide.

"Yes. And then I'll be ... Well, you know."

"Well, how long do you have?" Spoony asked.

"Not long I'm afraid," Pinky said, gaining confidence. "You see, once the symptoms start, it's just a matter of ..."

"What symptoms?"

"Loss of sensory integrity."

"What?"

More sure of himself now, Pinky went on. "All the senses start to short out. You know hearing, smelling."

"I've never heard of anything like that," Spoony said suspiciously.

"It's new," Pinky said.

"So you're telling me all your senses are going haywire! You say your hearing and your smelling and your vision and your taste ..." Spoony stopped in midsentence. A look of enlightenment came into his eyes. Then they narrowed as if he might be attempting to understand some revelation. Finally, as Pinky jabbered on, an expression of peace settled across Spoony's face. Perhaps his refusal to cook had gone on long enough. Maybe he was being offered a way to return to the bosom of his friends, a way to simply put things back as they were. Whatever his thoughts, they went unnoticed by Pinky. He was going on tearfully about how his sweet wife, the love of his life, now smelled to him like creamed corn.

Spoony turned to him and offered his hand. "Yes, yes, quite tragic," he said, with a faint smile. "And what you said about the soup, let's ... forget it."

"Yes, let's forget it," Pinky said happily.

When Pinky returned to the TV room, he plopped into a chair and let out a long breath. "He bought it," he said.

That evening the camp cook went back to his saucepans. The members were unusually quiet as we gathered in the kitchen for drinks. All eyes were on Spoony as he began preparing dinner. But Spoony was quiet too. He tiptoed around the room as if he might be afraid of spoiling his return to the fraternity of the club. But then Pogo began ribbing one of the newer members about not making a shot all morning. I glanced over at Spoony. He was grinning appreciatively. Soon the level of noise and laughter rose as the men relaxed into a familiar old pattern. Someone had contributed some Georgia quail to the larder, and Spoony rubbed them with rosemary and garlic and flambéed them in cognac. There were also steamed asparagus and garlic grits. When dinner was put on the table, we all went at it like jackals. All except for Pinky who pretended to only pick at his plate. But when Spoony's back was turned, he wolfed down huge mouthfuls. After a dessert of rice pudding with bourbon sauce, we pushed back our chairs. Roach Patton lit a cigar. The conversation turned, as usual, to weather and waterfowl. Finally, someone broke the spell.

"Well, those dishes aren't going to wash themselves." The camp cook immediately stood up and started toward the door. But when he reached it, he stopped. Then, as if he had just at that moment remembered his apron, he turned, facing the men seated at the long table, and began fidgeting with the apron strings. Beagle saw him first.

"Absolutely wonderful dinner, Spoon!" he called out, leaning back in his chair.

"Oh, you don't mean that," the camp cook said, blushing with pleasure. "Do you?"

Beaver Tale

From *Shooting Sportsman*

At the Old River Rod and Gun, Bloody Mary Society and Gentlemen's Club our battle with Mother Nature had gone on for decades. On our side of the conflict were twelve mostly inept club members and an assortment of incompetent hired help. Mother Nature's team was made up of rot, decay, creeping vegetation, and the fury of the elements. She had the edge.

Contrary to what many people think, nature is not nice. Oh sure, it sometimes seems that way. Granted, hiking in Yellowstone on a crisp, blue day, one might get that impression. There, on some high mountain trail, with the smell of lodge pole pine in your nose and wildflowers under your feet, it's easy to believe the whole outdoors is simply there for our pleasure. Try it in winter.

The truth is, this is a hostile world where man is concerned. We come into it naked and defenseless. To survive, we must make for ourselves a sheltered space. To prosper, we must actually bend the environment to our purposes. Don't misunderstand me. We are obliged to protect and preserve nature. After all, she is the unique bubble we inhabit and on which our very lives depend. But some of us oversimplify things. If nature sustains us, it must be good, right? Wrong. Mother Nature is neither good nor bad; she simply is. And if anything, she's evenhanded. She shows as much concern for the welfare of the worm as she does for the apple.

At the Old River our battle with the old girl was ceaseless. In summer, cedar and broom sedge appeared around the edges of our fields. These and other invasions could only be beaten back with regular bush hogging. With every passing season, the lodge seemed to settle a little farther down and to starboard, as if the ground were reaching up to pull the old structure into its bosom. In spring, the river boiled out of its banks and clawed at our levees, threatening to turn the property back into the old river channel it had once been.

But those were minor in comparison to the main conflict. That took place in the bottom where we hunted ducks. This was a place we had to defend at all costs, our Masada, our Alamo.

A small clear creek ran through the middle of the bottom, providing a year-round water source. Each spring we planted corn, millet, and milo there. This crop was cultivated, fertilized, and nurtured through the summer months. In autumn, if things went according to plan, the water control box at the lower end of the bottom was closed. The creek was allowed to back up and flood the ripe grain. Ideally the water was brought to a level a few inches below each ear of corn or head of grain, just where a duck likes it.

Perhaps critters are getting smarter, not necessarily in the Darwinian way, but in the way they interact with man, the way pheasants learn to run rather than fly when hunters are in a field and ducks learn to feed at night after shooting hours. Maybe over the generations animals can pass down knowledge about humankind in their DNA, or whatever. Until finally you've got a critter that can foil you at every turn.

One spring a new beaver showed up in the bottom. True to his nature, he set to work trying to turn the place into a shallow lake, suitable only for carp, turtles, and members of his own species. To do this, he constructed a dam of sticks and mud across the narrow lower end.

At first, we didn't take the challenge seriously. We'd had beavers before. We shouldered our grubbing hoes and shovels and destroyed the dam within an hour. Then we stood back and watched the water flow through, pleased with ourselves. But the next morning, the dam had been rebuilt. Of course we cleared it out again. The next morning the narrow gap was again packed with fresh mud and sticks. Again we cleared it. And again he rebuilt it. We set out a half-dozen traps but had no luck. They remained untouched.

One moonlight night Pogo Walters and Roach Patton sat up all night on the main levee with a varmint rifle. The next morning Pogo said, "We never saw hide nor hair of him. That's one cagey rascal!"

Since they had brought along a box of saltines, a can of Cheese Whiz, and two six packs, I was doubtful of the whole enterprise from the beginning. Later Roach admitted they might have been playing the guitar and singing a little too loudly.

As time passed, the problem became more serious. Grain won't grow underwater. Without a grain crop, we'd have no duck season. Yet everything we tried failed. The strain was beginning to show on some members; in fact, some were at the breaking point.

At about that time an incident took place that has become part of outdoor folklore. It has been told and retold in freezing duck blinds and around flickering hearths until it has entered the realm of myth. The tale has taken on other guises and other forms but always enough of the original remains for it to be recognizable. I was there, and this is what happened.

We stood on the levee that Sunday afternoon surveying the beaver's work. The dam had been rebuilt once more. Water was again backing up, edging toward the precious green seedlings. In a few hours the plants would be inundated. Pinky Lipman and some of the other members had spent all weekend at the club. It seemed they'd torn the dam out Friday afternoon and again Saturday afternoon. Each time the beaver had rebuilt it.

Pinky paced the levee nervously, muttering to himself. His cheeks, ordinarily a rosy pink, were fiery red. Suddenly he snapped his fingers.

"I'll teach that S.O.B!" he said.

He opened the back of his pickup topper and, after rummaging around a few minutes, came out with what appeared to be a stick of dynamite.

"So you want to play, huh?" he yelled in the direction of the dam. "So you want to play with Pinky Lipman?" he taunted. "Okay then, it's hard ball!"

Pinky pulled out his Zippo Windproof and lit the fuse. With a grunt, he tossed the dynamite in a high arc. It sailed end over end out over the beaver pond and stuck up right in the middle of the dam, its fuse hissing.

"There, you S.O.B!" he yelled. "Now we'll see, won't we?"

Just then Pinky's black Lab pup, Prince Rupert of Aberdeen, bounded out of the back of the truck and charged down the levee. For a moment, none of us grasped the consequences of this event. Then it seemed to dawn on all of us at once. Each of us took a step backward.

Then the seriousness of the situation hit Pinky.

"No, no!" he yelled. "Sit! Sit! Staaaaay!

Desperately, he blew several blasts on his whistle. But as every Lab owner knows, shock collars aside, once a Lab gets out of rock-throwing range that is past the distance where his master might inflict pain on him, he does exactly as he pleases. Prince Rupert reached his mark. He took the stick of dynamite in his teeth, the fuse burning, and loped happily up the levee toward us. We scattered like a covey of Georgia quail, all except Pinky. He seemed to be frozen in place.

"Run, Pinky!" I yelled.

"Run where?" he screamed. "He's bringing the damn thing right to me!"

ALAN PHILLIPS

I'll admit I didn't see the actual explosion. I did, however, hear it from some distance away. It was surprising what a great distance I had put between myself and Pinky by the time the dynamite went off. When I heard the blast, I turned and started back, not knowing what horrible scene awaited me.

What I found was a great commotion around the back end of Pinky's truck. He was sitting alone on the tailgate, surrounded by a concerned group of club members. Miraculously unharmed, Prince Rupert lay under the vehicle, peering out suspiciously. The group looked at me as if I were expected to say something important.

"Are you okay, Pink?" I asked.

Pinky didn't answer. His eyes were as large as dinner plates.

"Can you hear me?"

He didn't answer. The whistle was still in his mouth. He was blowing it, making a little squeaking sound.

"Squeak, squeak, squeak."

"Give me the whistle, Pinky."

"Squeak, squeak."

I pried it loose from his fingers.

Then he began making a little sound with his lips.

"Squeak, squeak."

"Are you all right?"

"Squeak."

Prince Rupert was unhurt. From his place under the vehicle, he looked out warily, now and then barking at the large recently made hole a few yards away.

Both of them had been lucky. Thankfully, the dog hadn't been quite finished in deliver to hand. As it turned out, he had dropped the dynamite eight or ten feet in front of his master and trotted away. That gave Pinky a chance to roll into a bar ditch and avoid the bulk of the blast.

Pinky didn't show up at the club for several weekends after the incident. I suppose his anger toward the beaver had cooled. Or perhaps he needed time to contemplate his life up to that point and decide what changes he might make in the way he lived the balance of it. A close call will make a man think about such things. Most of the other members lost their hostility too.

A local teenage boy was found who needed a summer job. He happened along when he was most needed, as people sometimes do. Each morning, through autumn, the boy was instructed to check the bottom. If the dam had been rebuilt, he was paid to tear it out again. He was a very patient boy, not prone to fits of rage.

Mother Nature frustrated us again that year by giving us an unusually mild winter. The big flights of ducks didn't come down from the north until well into the season. And when they arrived, the food on the refuge was adequate to keep them there. Very few left for the surrounding fields and bottoms.

Pinky didn't finish Prince Rupert's training. The dog was never taught to properly deliver to hand. Rupert always dropped a duck about ten feet in front of Pinky and then got back into his dog box. On a really good hunt, he'd make a little pile of birds out there. Pinky said he preferred to leave well enough alone.

So the beaver lived on, and the battle continued. And it continues to this day, perhaps not with that beaver but with one of his progeny. I suppose such confrontations will go on for a thousand generations, or as long as his species and man inhabit this green sphere.

Other catastrophes awaited us at the Old River. There was the year of the drought, when the place was turned into a dust bowl and our crops simply dried up and blew away. And there was the time the river topped the main levee, inundating the lodge. But these things are to be expected. Since man was expelled from Eden, our lot has been harsh. And Mother Nature is not in the habit of making things easy for us.

7

The Perfect Member

From *Shooting Sportsman*

At the Old River Rod and Gun, Bloody Mary Society and Gentlemen's Club, the word was out. The news was being circulated around all the duck hunting clubs that ringed the big refuge: a certain Dr. P. Horace Bloodworth had recently retired from Johns Hopkins and relocated to our area. Dr. Bloodworth was still a relatively young man and quite active in his favorite outdoor sport, duck hunting. He would be shopping for a new club membership.

The doctor's resumé was notable. It was said that he enjoyed carpentry, electrical work, plumbing, watercourse engineering, and other "hands on" hobbies, and his workshop and collection of tools were first rate. Furthermore, he kept several skilled workmen on salary to assist in whatever project he undertook. For example, he and his crew had added a recreation room to the lodge at his former club on the Chesapeake Bay at no cost to the members. He was able to afford such extravagances thanks to his family's great fortune, obtained from their wholesale liquor business and chain of sporting goods stores. In the medical field, the doctor had a fine reputation due to his dual specialties, the treatment of frostbite and the care of shotgun wounds.

The news was hardly out when Flywheel Smith, president of the neighboring Big Bottom Club, called our president, Deacon Maxwell.

"Lay off! He's ours!" he said.

"Lay off what? I don't know what you're talking about."

"Oh, yes you do. Dr. Bloodworth. He's ours!"

"What do you mean yours?"

"I've already been in contact with the man, and he'll be coming out this weekend to tour our place. So you can just butt out!"

"Well, maybe he'll want to shop around a little before making a decision."

There was silence on the line as Flywheel thought this over.

"Flywheel? You still there?" the Deacon asked.

"You're going down, Maxwell!" he shouted and hung up.

It was autumn, and the duck hunters in our area watched the national weather reports with great interest. Early blizzards and snows in the Midwest and plains states typically brought waterfowl south ahead of schedule. When the big numbers arrived before winter set in, food planted on the refuge often proved insufficient. This sent the birds foraging in the surrounding fields and river bottoms ... creating excellent opportunities for duck hunting.

As the first frosts came and the walnuts started falling, Pinky Lipman, our vice president, received a note from Van Leer Randolph IV, secretary of the Magnolia Club.

Dear Lipman,

I am writing to inform you that we have decided to offer Dr. Horace Bloodworth an invitation to become a member here at the Magnolia Club. Considering the man's reputation and standing, we feel that he'll fit in very well with our illustrious membership. Furthermore, it turns out the lovely Mrs. Bloodworth is related to our treasurer, Bobo Harrison. Bobo's grandfather was Mrs. Bloodworth's sister in-law's third cousin's uncle's oldest nephew. So, you see there is a close family connection. I am notifying you and the other hunting clubs in the area to save you the trouble of contacting the doctor.

On October 15 the water structures were closed at the Old River, and the creek was allowed to back up and flood the corn and millet in the lower fields. The season hadn't yet begun, but members began showing up on Saturday afternoons to look at the ducks or what might better be termed "look for the ducks," since as yet, there weren't any. But we'd had autumns like this one before. We remained hopeful. Through the Deacon's considerable business connections, he was able to meet Dr. Bloodworth. However, when he invited him to spend an afternoon touring our property, the doctor became quite vague on the subject and gave the impression he had never heard of our club. But the Deacon was not a man easily insulted or put off. After several more attempts, he persuaded the doctor to visit the Old River on the Saturday before opening day ... and to stay for dinner.

"Ahhh, yes, I'm thinking of an autumn menu," Spoony Odom said. He entwined the fingers of his very small hands together and gazed at the ceiling. "And perhaps I'll finish with a sherry custard," he declared with a knowing smile. Spoony was easily the best cook at any hunting or fishing camp in the area. He probably thought the doctor could be seduced with nothing more than one of his duck dinners. Several members conferred by telephone that week and carefully planned the other details of the visit.

It was promising to be a cold winter. A sizable number of birds had arrived on the big refuge by then, and we heard reports that some of them had started moving into the neighboring river bottoms. At the Old River we had done everything to make ready for the season and the arriving waterfowl. The blinds were brushed, the dog stands were shored up, and the lower fields were flooded. But we still hadn't seen a single duck.

A few days later, Roy "Magnum" Parnell, secretary-treasurer of the Hard Core Club, wearing his camouflage sports jacket, barged into the Deacon's office and confronted him, "I hear you're going to be wining and dining this Bloodworth fellow!"

"What do you mean wining and dining?"

"I mean buttering him up!"

"I don't know anything about buttering up."

"Look, I've heard all about it, and I know Odom's a great cook. But I've got ducks! Bloodworth visited our place the other day and saw a boatload of birds! Any day now, he'll be calling and begging us for a membership!"

"Oh, yeah? Are you sure he'll want to spend the season in that fleabag clubhouse of yours? A man could get bitten by a rat!"

"Oh, yeah? How many ducks did you shoot at your place last year?"

"None of your damn business!"

The chosen Saturday afternoon arrived at the Old River. It was a blue-sky day ... with not a duck in sight. The Deacon and Pogo Walters had been selected to give the doctor the tour of the property since the Deacon was an excellent talker and Pogo was an unusually pleasant person. During the tour, they placed much emphasis on the fishing opportunities. Then the three of them joined the other members on the reservoir boat dock for a cocktail. We kept our guest there as long as possible since watching the sun go down over our reservoir was a fine sight.

When the sun dipped below the water, the Deacon announced that we should adjourn to the lodge. After we were seated at the long kitchen table, Spoony brought out the first course, winter squash soup. Brother Harley Phipps was asked to say grace, which he did with great sincerity and detail.

Then came grilled mallard breasts with currant sauce, garden green beans, and roasted truffle potatoes. Spoony fussed and fretted at the stove all during dinner, adding more of this or that to his sauce and then putting another little dab on the doctor's plate. "I think this has more earth tones, don't you?" he asked each time.

As planned, the Deacon and Melvin Creamclot, two of our best storytellers, each told one of his best and funniest tales. The doctor seemed to enjoy them very much. When the sherry custard was finished, we looked expectantly at our guest, waiting for his opinion on the food.

"I must say, the food and the fellowship have both been excellent!" he said.

"Gentlemen, let us retire to the parlor for cigars!" the Deacon announced with growing confidence. The "parlor" was usually called the TV room, but we went in and took seats

ALAN PHILLIPS

around the fire. Roach Patton lit a cigar. He was one of the younger members and had not yet been cut off by his doctor. But the smell of it gave things a nice, clubby air.

And then as certain of the members had planned, the final phase began. Here, all the stops were to be pulled out and the sale closed. The job was left to our member, Marvin J. Beagle, attorney-at-law. Beagle began in his most sincere and ingratiating voice, "Doctor, may I say that your reputation precedes you?"

"My reputation? Do you mean in medicine?"

"I'm sure your standing in that field is stellar, sir. But no, I am referring to your reputation as a wing shot."

"You are?"

"Ha, ha. Don't pretend you don't know what I'm talking about," Beagle said with a chuckle.

I had heard nothing about Dr. Bloodworth being a great wing shot and suspected that he really wasn't one. But what man doesn't enjoy being described that way?"

"Well, I guess you could say ..." the doctor began, obviously flattered.

"Gentlemen," Beagle said, looking around the room, "we may well be in the presence of the Bogardus of our generation, the Ripon."

"Oh, I wouldn't go that far, Mr. Beagle."

"Your modesty is admirable, Doctor."

"Are you sure you've got the right ...?"

I was starting to think Beagle should lighten up a little. But I didn't say anything.

"Okay, not another word. But sir, may I ask a favor? A man of your outdoor experience must be a storehouse of wonderful tales. Would you mind regaling us with one of your adventures?"

After much prodding, our guest agreed to tell us about a dove shoot he'd once experienced in Mexico.

"Sir, that was probably the finest account of a shooting venture I've ever been privileged to hear," Beagle gushed.

"Well, thank you," our guest replied, clearly pleased.

I was beginning to squirm in my chair. Beagle was spreading on the butter like a hungry man with only one biscuit.

"And where may I read your work?" he continued. "Surely you've been in the pages of some of the finer magazines, or perhaps you've published a volume or two that escaped my notice."

"No. But I'm glad you liked the story."

"Liked it? I was spellbound!"

"Yes, spellbound!" several others agreed.

Then Beagle rose and walked over to where our guest was sitting. "My dear friend," he began, taking the man's hand. Then he lowered his backside onto the sofa next to the doctor without loosening his grasp. "My dear friend, we here at the Old River have decided to extend the hand of fellowship and offer you an opportunity to become one of us. You have been judged by this band of stalwart brothers and found worthy. This is a letter of intent," Beagle said, producing a pen and a clipboard. "It merely states that you intend to purchase a membership within the prescribed period of time for the amount stipulated. I'm sure you'll agree the price is quite modest."

The doctor looked surprised. After a moment he said, "Thank you. But I'll have to think this over."

Not long after, our guest said he'd best begin the drive back to the city. We accompanied him to the door and onto the front porch. Each of us shook his hand except Beagle, who insisted on a hug. After a time, the doctor wriggled loose from Beagle's hold. Then we all stood on the porch and watched our prospective perfect member's taillights disappear up the road.

So the season came. It wasn't the worst season we'd ever had nor was it the best. We took some ducks but probably not as many as some of the other clubs in the area and certainly fewer than Magnum and the boys at the Hard Core Club. But Spoony's dinners were excellent that year, and the fellowship was outstanding. The old fireplaces blazed, and the late night story telling lasted longer than was prudent for early rising duck hunters.

It turned out that Dr. Bloodworth bought into one of those famous clubs in Arkansas. Apparently the distance was not a factor since he flew his own plane and the facility had an airstrip. I suppose the price of membership was pretty high. Certain clubs in our area were very upset. It was said that the members of the Magnolia Club were in shock. But at the Old River, we got over it pretty quickly. After all, we had muddled through good seasons and bad and would continue to muddle through. And to be truthful, there was another reason we didn't take it very hard. Remember the doctor's tale about his dove shoot in Mexico? He was the worst storyteller we'd ever heard.

A Sunflower Saga

From *Shooting Sportsman*

"Anything flying, Bob?" It was Doc Youngman, one of the club members. He was just arriving.

"A few," I said.

He stood out in the blazing September sun, loaded down with every kind of dove hunting paraphernalia imaginable. Shading his eyes, he peered into the shadows at me. "Just a few?" he repeated, sounding disappointed.

I had set up my stool under the row of hackberries and oaks that line the river. It was traditionally a good spot if you were quick enough to catch the doves coming over the treetops. And it was a damned site cooler than anywhere else. After all, it was September 1 in the South, opening day, and hot enough to blister a rock.

"There's plenty of time yet," I said a little irritably.

"Oh yes, plenty of time," he obliged.

ALAN PHILLIPS

He took a few steps into the shade and put down his folding chair and game bag as well as numerous other things I couldn't identify. Then he looked down at the oversized outdoor timepiece on his wrist. It was as big as a yo-yo.

"What time do you have?" he asked innocently.

"Three o'clock," I answered.

"Me, too," he said. Then he wiped his neck with a camo-patterned bandanna. "I know it's still early," he said off-handedly, "but hadn't the birds started flying by three o'clock last year?"

"I don't remember," I lied.

"It seems to me," he went on, "we had quite a few birds by three o'clock last year."

"Okay, look, Doc," I said, louder than I intended. "I've done everything here that can be legally done with a dove field. If there aren't any ..."

"Yes, of course. I know you've done your best," he said apologetically. "No one would blame *you* if the birds didn't show up."

For the average person, a dove hunt is a simple matter. You arrive with a shotgun and a stool, find a likely looking spot, sit down, and wait for a bird to fly over. But there's a lot more to this shindig than most trigger pullers know. For every hunt, there's a field. And for every field, there's some person who prepared it. Some unsung hero who, working alone and unappreciated, plowed and seeded, disked and reseeded, cut and burned, counted birds in the afternoons, and felt the onset of fear and anxiety as opening day neared. For five years, I was that person.

"Sunflower," Doc said, barging in on my thoughts.

"What?" I asked.

He was peering through a tiny set of straw-colored binoculars, surveying the field from one side to the other.

"Sunflower. That's what you should have planted out here, sunflower," he said. "Doves can't resist it. The last time I shot over sunflower, the birds were as thick as mosquitoes."

Before I could respond, we were interrupted by the sound of shotguns popping. A pair of low birds rocketed down the far edge of the field. There were reports from several hides, but the two doves sped on. They zigged and zagged, untouched, over hay rolls and weed patches as each hunter stood up and took his turn. Finally, the last man got to his feet. Clearing the top of his hay roll, he nailed the first bird out front in a halo of feathers. Then he bagged

ALAN PHILLIPS

the second one high overhead. Thank the Lord somebody out there could shoot. The best I could estimate, that gave us a miserable fourteen.

"Maybe they're starting to fly," Doc said hopefully. He picked up his gear and hurried away, his canteen, shotgun, and stool banging against each other and making strange music.

Who knows? If I'd ever been able to get in a crop of sunflower, the birds might have blacked out the sun. But probably not. The truth is, the Old River

Rod and Gun, Bloody Mary Society and Gentlemen's Club was never a hot spot for dove shooting. Our field looked perfect enough with its line of old trees edging the river, separating it from the high gravelly meadow. But for some reason, it was not a place where doves naturally gathered. In some areas, simply cutting a few rows of corn with a circular blade will bring in birds. Not in ours. It required much more effort.

Since the ground was always muddy in the low places surrounding the field until early summer, we could never get a tractor in soon enough to plant a spring crop. That ruled out sunflower. I had to rely mostly on winter wheat from the preceding fall. My work started in early August, a month or so before opening day. My helper and I began by plowing and seeding some sections, burning some and leaving others standing. The idea was to keep grain on the ground constantly. The goal was to build a concentration of birds peaking, of course, on opening day. But no matter how many were feeding in the field up to then, success was never guaranteed. Let the smallest cool front move through, and the doves would disappear overnight. A neighboring farmer harvesting a cornfield might have the same effect.

Suddenly, two pairs topped the trees on the west boundary.

"Coming at you, Doc!" I shouted.

He was fifty yards away, trying to assemble a dove chair the size of a pup tent. He didn't seem to hear me.

"Doc! Birds! Doc!"

"What?" he asked, finally looking toward me.

"Never mind," I called out.

The four doves had already shot over him and into the middle of the field. There was a gunner hidden there every thirty yards. It sounded like Hood's charge at Franklin. The first two birds went down immediately. The second pair went into maneuvers, cutting and veering. Even hunters on the perimeter of the line were banging away, trying to poach a shot. Everybody wanted to pull the trigger. The third dove fell at the end of the field. The last one soared out of sight over the corn. What did that give us? Seventeen, eighteen?

My best year we shot 220 birds. I know, for thirty-five guns, that's only six each. But most of the good shots limited out that year. And even guests who couldn't shoot very well got two or three apiece. Another opening day, we shot 180 and another, 120. There was one year when no doves were anywhere in the area. Zero. I canceled the shoot.

Even with 120 birds, we could still hold our customary dinner at the old clubhouse. With the usual five or so non-shooting guests joining the hunters, the total for dinner was usually about forty. Okay, each hunter had to eat lots of rice and corn on the cob. But it's the romance of the thing that counts.

I glanced down at my watch. It was already four o'clock. If the big flights were coming, they'd better hurry. An attack of anxiety hit me. I decided to take a walk around the field. Unloading my shotgun, I broke it across my forearm and set out. Behind the first hay roll, I found two of our members' daugh-

ters, two girls whose fathers I had known for decades. They were college-aged young ladies now and of a certain type, the kind who had grown up around fishing and shooting. They weren't the only women in the field. Several wives were present. It was an opening day tradition. The two girls were seated in comfy shooting chairs. Between them was a cooler of diet soft drinks.

"Afternoon, girls," I said in a cheery voice.

"Hello, Mr. Bob," they answered, making me feel downright prehistoric. I remembered these two as children, sitting on the boat dock with cane poles

ALAN PHILLIPS

and catching bluegill. They were too small then even to take their own fish off the hook. Today, they were both wearing colorful bandannas around their necks with doves and quail on them and khaki outfits that looked like they were suited for a grand safari. One sported a straw cowboy hat and the other an Australian bushwhacker. The cowboy hat looked like it might have come from one of those shops around Jackson Hole. I was suddenly aware of the big sweat stains under my arms.

"Doing any good?" I asked.

"We've got two birds," one of them said, smiling. "Is it any better down where you are?"

"Well, no," I admitted.

"There's still plenty of time," the other remarked hopefully.

"Yes, there's plenty of time," I repeated, even though I wasn't so sure there was. "Good luck, ladies," I said as I started out to finish my rounds.

"Mr. Bob?" one of them said.

"Yes?"

"Daddy said to give you this."

She handed me a thin pamphlet. It was something distributed by our state wildlife agency. On the cover was a mourning dove in full flight. And below the drawing it read: *Planting and Harvesting Sunflower in Southern Dove Fields.* I cut my stroll short and went back to my stool.

Just as I was taking a long pull on my canteen, someone called out. "Down the road!" Good Lord, that meant me! I looked up and saw a half-dozen gray forms barreling up the tractor road, low and fast.

Okay, don't mess this up, I whispered to myself. *These may be the only birds you get.* That would later prove to be true.

The fact that I had set up my stool in the shade might have given me another advantage. I may have been harder to see in the shadows. I fought the urge to jump to my feet. Instead, I eased myself up like a cat. I did this instinctively, having no idea at the time (and I still don't) whether moving slowly makes one less noticeable to a bird on the wing. Anyway, they didn't see me. They continued hurrying up the road, swooping and turning, like a half-dozen outlaws who had just robbed a bank. Now or never. The lead dove was right over me. I suddenly realized how fast it was moving. But what is a liability for many shooters is sometimes an asset for me. I had no opportunity to muddy my head with calculations. There was only just time to shoot the gun, right or wrong. I swung the muzzles, and when they crossed an imaginary point ahead of the bird, I pulled the trigger. Down it came like a burned-out rocket. Then I ratcheted backward and picked up another. Quick! This one was higher up. I could only blot it out and fire. It hit the ground with a thump. Yes! A double! I felt a surge of pure joy. I'm not the kind of wing shot who routinely shoots doubles on mourning doves. I had almost forgotten how much fun dove shooting could be.

I sat down and watched as birds began coming in over the northwest corner. That was their usual pattern in late afternoon. Many of the best shots were positioned there, and while it lasted, they downed almost everything that came over the trees. But the doves never appeared in the big numbers I had hoped for. By six o'clock, some of the hunters started leaving the field. Looking hot and tired, they walked by me carrying stools, shell bags, coolers, and shotguns. No one had shot a limit. In fact no one had more than two or three birds. The diehards hung on for another half hour, but it didn't help much. I estimated that we had bagged about eighty doves. Not one of my best years.

The yard in front of the old farmhouse was crowded with people. A dozen or so card tables had been set up on the grass, each one with four folding chairs. On top of each table, the ladies had placed a Chinese lantern and a bouquet of field flowers and wheat straw. Some people had drinks in their hands. Others were starting to line up at the long serving table. Slick Lawson, our self-appointed executive chef, was busy giving orders to his teenage helpers. They darted in and out of the house carrying plates, utensils, and steaming pots of food. Then as the diners lined up, each plate was filled. There were corn on the cob, wild rice, scratch biscuits, and two small dove breasts, sautéed and dribbled with a red wine sauce.

The sun had just gone down behind the western rim, and the temperature had dropped noticeably, making it pleasant out. One of the ladies was going around lighting the Chinese lanterns. Doc Youngman was demonstrating one of those pocketknives with a dozen built-in gadgets. I tossed my plastic cup into one of the big garbage cans and started toward the food line.

"Psst, hey, Bob," someone said. I looked around to see who had called me, but in the failing light, I couldn't find anyone.

"Psst, Bob, over here."

It was Bill Gray, a tall shy man who was one of the founding members of

ALAN PHILLIPS

the club. He was standing in the near darkness at the edge of the lawn, half hidden behind a forsythia bush. In one hand he held a clear plastic cup of red wine. In the other, a paper plate with corn, rice, and two tiny dove breasts. I walked over.

"Yes, Bill," I said.

"Do you have a minute?"

"Sure."

He looked around the lawn to make sure no one else was in earshot, as if what he had to say was only for me to know.

"I just want to say one thing to you, Bob."

"What's that?"

Glancing from side to side again, he leaned in close until his face was barely an inch from mine.

"Sunflower," he whispered.

9

The Captain and The Grand Apparatus

"Men," the Captain began one morning, "what separates humankind from the beasts of the field?" He looked around the duck blind, searching our faces.

"I don't know, Captain," I said, answering, I assumed, for all of us.

That seemed to satisfy him. He paused a moment as if to gather his thoughts, then continued. "Some say it is man's ability to use tools that distinguishes him from the animals."

Pogo Walters yawned noticeably. Pinky Lipman fumbled with his thermos bottle. On the horizon, the first sliver of an orange sun appeared. It lit up the frosty cornstalks around our duck blind and sparkled on the water like amber.

The Captain went on, "But now we have discovered that a chimpanzee can take a twig and fish termites out of a hole. By definition, that twig is a tool. So, if an animal can use a tool, then how is man superior to it? And if he is superior, then in what way?"

No one answered.

"Boys," he continued a little louder, so as to be heard by all those present, "what elevates us from the apes is something much greater than the use of tools. It is a thing only mankind can accomplish. It is *invention*. We do not merely pick up a stick or stone and use it to some purpose. We are capable of changing that stick or stone, shaping it to our needs." Then he lowered the tempo and tone of his voice as if signing off on the evening news. "Man is a tinkerer, my boys, an inventor, and that is his highest calling."

In that gathering of building contractors, real estate agents, and insurance salesmen, opinions on such things were unusual. The Captain mostly had the floor to himself. However, Brother Harley Phipps expressed the view that it is man's immortal soul that separates him from the beasts. The Captain dismissed this as theology. He said it was a subject to be taken up on Sunday morning and not suited for the serious scientific exchange of the duck blind.

Of course, the Captain was a tinkerer, or what most people would call an inventor. When he retired from the U.S Navy after twenty-five years as an engineering officer, it seemed he had a lot of tinkering left in him. Soon after he joined the Old River Rod and Gun, Bloody Mary Society and Gentlemen's Club, he started right in inventing things. First, he built a directional duck blind. Next came a mechanical dog trainer. Then he built a wind-powered pond aerator, which worked pretty well ... except in a really high wind.

But all those things paled compared to the Captain's most famous invention. It wasn't that the Grand Apparatus was a great success if you define success in the usual way. The reason it became famous was because it was ... well, it was grand.

I remember the day the idea hit him, the very moment it sprang into his mind. It was one of those steamy August afternoons when heat hangs in the southern air like old draperies. The two of us were cleaning a dozen or so red ear and bluegill on the footbridge behind the lodge. The Captain had fished the reservoir with me that afternoon to try out a newly designed boat anchor. The little bridge was an ideal place for scaling fish. The water that ran under it was as pure and cold as any in the county. In the short distance from its source, where it bubbled out off a hillside a few yards upstream, to the bridge, it gained only a degree or two in temperature. The Captain had already remarked on how cold the water was.

I'd also noticed him glancing back at the lodge where the two of us and another member or two had spent the night before sweltering under the ancient ceiling fans.

Then the idea hit him. It came like a bolt of lightning from some distant place. Down that country road it came, striking fire off the limestone bluffs and glancing off the ancient sycamores until it struck the Captain between the eyes and poleaxed him like a Hereford steer. At that moment, his face froze, and he got to his feet.

"How cold do you think this water is?" he asked.

"I don't know, Captain," I answered.

Without a word, he turned and walked into the lodge. Returning with the thermometer from the first aid kit, he plunged it underwater and held it there. Then he read the tiny scale.

"Fifty-six degrees!" he announced.

He looked away to the horizon. Then in a voice aided in gravity by a barely detectable tremolo, he said, "I'm going to air-condition the lodge with spring water."

I was left alone that evening on the little footbridge. I cleaned the remaining fish to a chorus of frogs. The Captain had moved on to larger things. He was already at the kitchen table scribbling and sketching.

Over the next few weeks, the Apparatus began to take shape. Each weekend new pieces were added. The bulk of the thing was located in the front hall. It consisted of two huge truck radiators, almost shoulder high, bolted together, one behind the other. Woven in and around these were tangles of wire and copper tubing. Metal coils pointed in all directions. Several electric motors were employed as well as a surplus water pump from the State Flood Control Bureau. Connected to this machine was a maze of black stove pipe. This "duct work," as it was referred to, wound up and overhead into the separate rooms. Due to the machine's power requirements, the Captain had the electrical service for the lodge significantly upgraded.

Long before the Apparatus was started up, he enjoyed explaining it to the members. "We're not creating cold here," he said one day, pointing to one of the radiators. "Our machine does not follow the usual procedures of refrigeration. In fact, no refrigerant is employed." Removing the little screwdriver that he always kept clipped in his shirt pocket, he tapped a section of tubing. "We're merely borrowing cold," he said. "The fifty-six-degree temperature of the creek water is being moved indoors. Once indoors, the cold is extracted through our set of radiators." Then with a smile, he summed up, "Unburdened of its abnormal temperature, the water is then returned to the creek."

"Wouldn't it be easier to buy one or two of those window air conditioners?" Pinky Lipman asked.

"Why don't you leave the engineering to me, and I'll leave the copy machine selling to you?" the Captain snapped.

"Office equipment," Pinky replied, correcting him.

"Whatever," The Captain said.

When he announced that the Apparatus would be started up the following Saturday, almost all the club members drove out for the big event. We gathered in the front hall as the Captain made a few last adjustments. It was one of the hottest days of the summer. Most of us had decided to stay over and enjoy an evening of air-conditioned comfort. Finally, the Captain was ready. He looked around at the group and made a sweeping gesture toward the Apparatus.

"I dedicate this machine," he announced, "to man's ever-inquiring mind and to the ongoing pursuit of science."

"Amen," Brother Phipps intoned.

With a flourish, the Captain flipped the switch. The Apparatus sprang to life with a hum. Several of us grinned approvingly while the Captain very studiously adjusted a setscrew on the side of the machine. But just as Pogo Walters was congratulating him, the lights in the lodge dimmed. Then the floor began to vibrate. The next thing I knew the top of my head felt cold. When I reached up and touched it, I found that my hat was gone. It had been lifted right off my head. In fact, all our hats had been lifted into the air. Our collective headgear was swirling around the top of the room like the planets in a schoolhouse replica of the solar system. The whirl had also picked up scrap paper, a few dead insects, and all the notices from the bulletin board. Pogo's fedora was slapping against the high front window like a trapped bird looking for a way out. Then with a loud crash, the old buffalo head that hung over the front door fell to the floor. A new cloud of dirt and sawdust rose and was swept into the torrent. On impact, the animal's one remaining glass eye popped out and went bouncing down the hallway in high arcs. When it reached the back wall, it struck it and started back toward us. Hopping five or six feet in the air, the great glass orb circled the room. As it passed each of us, it glared mysteriously as if it wished to ask some question that it couldn't articulate. At that moment, I heard Pinky's voice behind me.

"It's stuck, it's stuck!" he yelled.

He was pulling at the front door.

"Hurry up!" Pogo shouted.

"Get out of the way!" the Deacon bellowed, shoving them both aside. He lowered his shoulder and crashed his sizable mass against the door. It gave way with the sound of splintering wood. He hurried through it, followed by the rest of the members.

Then I saw the Captain at the opposite end of the room. He was making his way toward the switch on top of the machine. The torrent whipped at his clothes as Pinky's porkpie swooped down and slapped the side of his face. With his arms outstretched, he edged toward the Apparatus. The scream of the motors was ascending to a higher and higher pitch.

Then the Captain saw me. "Get out!" he shouted.

I stood frozen, not sure of what I should do. I had spent more weekends at the club with the Captain than the other members. I considered him a friend. I wanted to help.

"Get out of here, sailor!" he yelled, seeming to forget where he was. Then he called out over the wail of the machine, "She might bloooooooow!"

I turned and hurried out the door. When I reached the front yard, I encountered the entire club membership huddled behind Pogo's giant SUV, all of them hatless. With their balding heads, they looked like a nest of baby birds. I had no sooner taken my place among them when the Captain ran out onto the porch. His hair stood straight up as if he were in the act of falling off a building.

"I can't turn it off!" he yelled.

"He can't turn it off," Pogo repeated.

I had never seen the Captain at a loss. None of us moved. He stood for a moment frozen in indecision. Then the solution hit him. "The main breaker!" he called out as he started around the side of the lodge. We fell in behind him like a pack of schoolchildren in a fire drill. Up the back steps we went and onto the back porch where the new and much larger electrical service panel had been installed. "We've got to shut her down!" the Captain shouted. Jerking open the metal door, he reached for the big handle at the top marked MAIN. He pulled. Then he pulled again. "It's fused! It's fused shut!" he yelled. The Deacon grabbed the handle and leveraged his considerable heft against it. It didn't budge. "Somebody get a hammer!" The Captain shouted.

"He needs a hammer!" Pogo repeated.

Just as Pinky was breaking toward the tool shed, there was a loud boom followed by crackling and popping sounds. The Captain seemed to know immediately where the sound was coming from. We followed him down the back porch steps and onto the back lawn and the edge of the lake. On a big pole behind the lodge was a steel can the size of a Lincoln, the transformer for half the county. Now in the approaching twilight, it was the source of a dazzling display of skyrockets, Roman candles, and fireballs. Many of the burning missiles shot out over the lake in spectacular arcs, then exploded into thousands of tiny sparks, reflected on the mirror-still water. It was as if we were celebrating some Italian holiday on Lake Como. We stood transfixed, unable to look away and not knowing if it would be improper to say that it was beautiful. After a few minutes, the display slowed, and the transformer itself caught fire. The screaming noise inside the lodge descended. Down went the pitch, lower and lower like the final groans of a wounded animal. Finally, there was only a low rumble and then nothing. A small fire flickered atop the transformer.

Autumn came that year at the Old River bringing, as always, new enthusiasm about the approaching waterfowl season. The duck blinds and dog stands were re-brushed and put in good repair. In October, the water gates were closed, and water was allowed to back up, flooding the corn and native grasses in the bottom along the river. Soon there was a fire in the parlor fireplace. The subject of air-conditioning was far from anyone's mind.

The Apparatus was never started up again. Someone, I suspect the Captain himself, disconnected its wiring. There were other inventions over the years like the heated boot dryer and the automatic decoy washer, but never again anything so ambitious. Long after the Captain had passed away, the machine still stood there in the front hall. Over time it became a convenient place to lay waders, drape wet hunting coats, and lean boat paddles. We paid it no attention ... unless some curious guest inquired about it. Then one of us would be obliged to tell the story all over again.

10

Moonlight Gamble

(Mallards in the Mist)

The snow had started falling again. The flakes, lit by the street lamp outside my office window, looked as large as dinner plates. As I gazed out at this latest installment of a weeklong arctic blast, I wondered what the streets would be like on my way home. For six days, the temperature had hovered between zero and ten degrees. It had almost brought our southern city to a standstill. As I was gathering up my hat and coat to leave, the phone rang.

"It's Mr. Maxwell," the receptionist said.

Mr. Maxwell, or the Deacon, was a longtime hunting companion and president of the Old River Rod and Gun, Bloody Mary Society and Gentlemen's Club. He was, in fact, a deacon at the First Presbyterian Church. But I'd never seen him display much religion ... except in the pursuit of waterfowl.

"I'll take it," I told her. "Hello, Deacon," I said.

"Get your gear together," he said, ignoring my greeting.

"Get my gear together? If you're talking about duck hunting, you're dreaming. The whole country's frozen up. There's no open water for a hundred miles."

"There are rumors afloat, my friend," he said in a low voice. "I have it on good authority that No. 5 is open. It's also rumored that several hundred mallards were using it yesterday morning."

That made sense. No. 5 was a pool of several acres that backed up behind a levee. Our all-weather spring, which began a few hundred yards upstream, ran into it and went out the lower end through a spillway. The temperature of the water at the springhead was fifty-five degrees year-round. No. 5 was always the last place at the club to freeze.

"It's perfect," the Deacon said. "The food on the refuge is probably covered up with snow. All the lakes are frozen. Where else are the ducks going to go?"

"South, if they have any sense," I answered.

ISTOCK

"Rumor has it that there are still some ducks around," the Deacon countered. I didn't ask where the rumor came from. He was usually reluctant to reveal his sources.

"But there's no blind at No. 5 pond," I said. "There aren't even any weeds to hide in.

"I think I know how to solve that," he said. "What do you say?"

"I don't know, Deacon. We'd be getting a late start. And there's no guarantee the ducks will still be there."

"There are no guarantees in life or in waterfowling, my friend," he said with a prophetic tone. I was defenseless.

"Well, all right."

"Great. I'll pick you up at 7:00 p.m."

At precisely 7:00 the Deacon's old International Scout crept up my driveway. I threw my gear in the back, opened the passenger's side door, and slid in. The overhead light lit his face.

"The interstate's a mess," he said. "The radio says the whole thing's a sheet of ice. It may take us a while."

"I know. That's what I've been trying to tell you," I said. "I'm not sure we ought to ..."

But we were already backing out the driveway. Protest was futile. Sure enough, the interstate was slow going. Traffic was plodding west at about ten mph. The snow had stopped, but the big trucks had pounded it into another layer of ice. Several cars were stuck nose-down in the snowy ditches beside the westbound lane. I could see the flashing red lights of emergency vehicles in the distance.

We put the Scout in four-wheel drive, locked the front hubs, and proceeded west at a crawl. The duck camp was sixty miles away. A short distance out of town, the snow started up again. At times it was so thick, we had to pull over and wait it out. What usually took one hour took us almost three. We drove through the club gate at the stroke of midnight.

"Let's see if those ducks are still there," I said.

"Yes," the Deacon answered, lowering his voice.

Stopping well short of the main levee, we quietly unlatched the doors and stepped out onto the new fallen snow. The moon was bright now and the sky clear and black. Everything was perfectly still, and the moonlight on the fresh white blanket seemed to light up the whole countryside. The first thing I noticed was a column of steam rising several hundred feet into the air directly over No. 5 pond.

"She's still open," the Deacon whispered.

A moment later we were crouching on top of the main levee looking down. There, half hidden in the rising water vapor, were about 500 mallards. They were crowded onto no more than two acres of water. The whole flock seemed to spot us at once and thundered into the air. We looked at each other questioningly, wondering if we had done the right thing. Should we have rallied them? The birds headed out over the river toward the refuge.

"They'll be back," the Deacon said.

"Maybe," I answered.

"Well, I say we play out our hand. Are you with me?"

"All right," I said. "But just supposing they do come back, how do we hunt this spot without a duck blind?"

"I've got that all figured out," he said.

A few minutes later we were inside the decoy house. I was holding a flashlight and watching the Deacon push aside lumber, goose silhouettes, old inner tubes, and rolls of roofing.

"What are we looking for?" I asked.

"You'll see," he answered, out of breath.

Then under a sheet of plywood and a sneak boat with a hole it, he found it.

"Here it is!" he said.

There in the corner sat a rusty little structure made of welded angle iron and shaped like an elongated box. The little contraption stood about four feet high, four feet deep, and eight feet long. Its sides were covered with broken chicken wire.

"What is it?" I asked.

"It's a stick up."

"A what?"

"You know, a hide, a temporary, a portable blind."

"It doesn't look like it would hide anybody."

"Well sure, not now. It has to be brushed."

"Brushed? Deacon, it's 1:00 a.m."

"Hey, I say we're in too deep to quit now, my friend. We can rope it to the top of the Scout and drive down to the cane thicket. We'll brush it right there in the field. Then we'll put her back on top and take her to No. 5."

"Well, where do you sit in this thing?"

"You don't," he said, "you squat."

I lifted one corner of the blind. It weighed about as much as a small automobile.

"What's it made of?" I asked.

"It's old," the Deacon said. "They built things to last back then."

Two and a half hours later, we were moving carefully down the narrow levee that formed the west bank of No. 5 pond. Strapped on top of the Scout was our newly brushed portable blind. The Deacon stopped at the water's edge. We wrestled it off the top of the vehicle and set it down in the mud on the north side of the water.

"If the wind starts up it's likely to be from the north," he said, his breath frosty. "This will put the birds out in front of us."

What birds? I thought.

There was no sign of a duck anywhere. If they were coming back, I could see no indication of it.

"I think it looks good," the Deacon announced, admiring our work.

I looked down at the freshly caned little structure. It represented two and a half hours of work in freezing temperatures. In the process, we had acquired two bruised shins and a mashed finger. Along with the harrowing and nerve-racking drive from the city, we now had almost eight hours invested in this hunt. I'd worked hard for ducks before, but it seemed we were putting an unusual number of chips on the table. The wager was getting high. We threw out a dozen decoys. It was too late to quit now.

Back at the cabin, we stoked up the fire and went to bed. It was 3:00 a.m. At five the alarm went off. I considered turning over and begging off. But the Deacon was already up.

"You can't get on the train if you're not at the station!" he called from the kitchen. When it came to duck hunting, his commitment was total. He didn't require coffee or food. The Deacon often hunted all day on nothing but a glass of tap water. Against his wishes, I brewed a pot of coffee and filled a thermos.

The moon was still high as we made our way toward the main levee. It was even colder now, probably down near zero. But up ahead I could see the column of water vapor rising high in the air. No. 5 still hadn't frozen. We opened the little door at the back of our blind and crawled in. There was, of course, no place to sit. After trying various positions, we settled down on our knees in the icy mud. There was no other way to arrange oneself. In a few minutes, contact with the ground began to take effect. I could feel the cold, wet earth drawing the warmth out of me. The discomfort of squatting on my knees only added to the misery.

Looking over my right shoulder, I could see blind No. 7, or The Ritz as we called it, silhouetted in the darkness. Inside were comfortable benches, a shooting platform, and even a charcoal heater. But the Ritz was useless now. A hundred yards too far north, it was stuck in a frozen expanse of snow-covered ice.

There was a very real possibility that none of this was going to pay off. But that was the way of things. Waterfowl don't always follow the rulebook. The birds had possibly rafted up somewhere on the big water, or perhaps they'd even started south. I knew the Deacon was thinking the same thing.

"Well, we're legal," he whispered as he pointed a flashlight at his wristwatch.

My mind began to drift. I was back at the shack, stretched out in a warm bunk with nothing ahead of me but days and days of delicious sleep.

"There!" Deacon whispered.

Suspended in the mist out over the pond were four green heads and a susie. By the time I could get my old A5 to my shoulder, he had dropped two of the drakes. The remaining birds backpedaled and rose quickly into the steam. I was able to bring down a third green head before they disappeared.

"We're going to shoot some ducks today, Ranger!" the Deacon shouted.

"Yes, I believe we are!" I answered as we slapped our gloved hands together.

He was still fumbling to reload when he looked over my shoulder and shouted, "Shoot 'em, damnit!"

I turned and took an easy double, a pair of big drakes suspended in the mist like Christmas tree ornaments. These birds were hanging on the wind like targets in a shooting gallery.

"Green heads only!" I said.

It was the kind of morning when a man can pick and choose his shots. If one drake can service ten susies, then we would do our part for the nesting effort. Then I realized the air was filled with birds, mostly big late season mallards but also widgeons and gadwalls. The column of water vapor was like a beacon, rising 200 feet in the air. The plume could probably be seen for miles in every direction, and it said, "Open water." Here were all the ducks we'd seen the night before plus hundreds more, all trying to come into our pond.

Soon we had our mallards and were looking for widgeons to finish out our limits. We caught two widgeon drakes straight out front and then a moment later two more. It was all over. We had limited out in less than thirty minutes.

We crawled out the back of the little blind and stood up, stretching our cramped muscles. Hundreds of ducks were still in the air. But now we were visible, and they were catching the wind and flaring away out of shooting range. We slung the heavy birds over our shoulders and started toward the levee.

Then I saw Pogo Walters peeping out of the top of the Ritz. He and his hunting partner had slipped in during the excitement.

"Hey, Pogo!" I called out, "the ducks are over here."

"I can see that!" he answered.

He got my meaning. As we started up the levee, he and his guest exited the back of the Ritz and began hurrying toward our little temporary blind.

"They'll limit out too," the Deacon said. "They should be done in thirty minutes."

"Let's wait for them at the shack. We'll all go up to the highway and get some breakfast," I suggested.

"Yes," the Deacon agreed. "And we'll make Pogo pay the bill. He'll owe us after this."

At the top of the levee we looked back at No. 5 pond. I stomped and shuffled my frozen feet, trying to return some feeling to them. Hundreds of ducks were again circling high in the mist above the little blind.

"What a morning!" I said.

The Deacon appeared to be deep in thought. Finally, after a long silence he said, "You know ... I'm not a gambler in the usual way."

"I know, Deacon," I said. His profession was advising other people on how to plan their estates and invest their money. He was anything *but* a gambler.

"But, Ranger Bob," he said, "did this one pay off or what?"

11

The Morning After

"Where in the hell are you going?" Pinky asked sleepily.

"To the dove field," I whispered.

"The dove field? What for?"

"To shoot."

"What time is it?" he asked, squinting at me.

"It's seven."

"Well ... don't expect me to go with you," he said. Then he turned toward the wall and pulled his sleeping bag up around his ears.

I stood in the bunkroom of the old lodge assembling my gear. As I picked up my dove chair, ammo bag, and water jug, a half dozen snores emanated from the bunks around me. An alarm went off somewhere in the half darkness. It was immediately silenced. Its owner, after a surprisingly short time, again took up his snoring. I put on my wide-brimmed straw hat and eased out the front door, being careful not to let the screen door slam. The morning sun was still below the tree line as I made my way down the levee.

It was September 2, the day after opening day of dove season. As usual, several members of the Old River Rod and Gun, Bloody Mary Society and Gentlemen's Club had slept over, vowing to get up bright and early and shoot the dove field again the next morning. But the post-hunt celebration had gone a little long. It seemed I was the only participant.

Opening day had been a good one. Thirty guns, including men, women, and several teenagers, had bagged 225 birds. That comes out to 7 1/2 birds each. No, it wasn't a slaughter. But some of the better shots limited out. Almost everyone drew blood. For our locale and our little club, it had been a good day. We'd put in some hard work on the field, not to mention money, and for once, the little critters had arrived on time.

I walked through the field, stopping occasionally to pick up an empty shell case or soda pop can. Yesterday the place had been as hectic as an English driven shoot. Now it was like a high school gym the morning after the prom.

"Hey, Bob," someone said.

I jumped a little. Who else could be awake and moving about at this time of the morning? Winton, our oldest club member, looked out from behind the first hay roll. He was wearing a washed-out shell vest and a khaki porkpie. Tufts of white hair stuck out from under the hat's edge, making him look like the scarecrow in *The Wizard of Oz*. In his lap was a vintage Lefever.

"Hey, Winton," I said. "What are you doing out here?"

"I thought I'd see if any birds are still around."

"You're up early."

"Oh, no. I get up early every morning."

He had disappeared the evening before at six o'clock, right after the shoot, foregoing the drinks, dinner, and party. No one paid much attention since Winton had stopped participating in that kind of thing years ago. Late in life, the old boy had become downright sensible. At the last annual club business meeting, he had refused his second portion of pork barbecue. I assumed he had driven back to the city the night before and gone to bed at a reasonable hour.

"See anything flying?" I asked.

"Not yet."

"Anybody else out here?"

"Just you and me."

"Well, I don't expect to see a lot of action," I said.

The second day never measured up to the opener. Winton and I knew that. We stood there together, staring across the meadow at the trees on the other end, considering our chances.

"Well, let's give it an hour or two," he proposed.

"I'm willing," I said. "But there are only two of us, and this is a damned big field."

"I know," he agreed. "But listen. Why don't you get about forty yards from the east end, and I'll get about forty yards from this end. We'll be back to back. I'll look west and you look east."

"What about the birds that come in from the sides?"

"What about them?"

"We'll be twisting our necks like that girl in *The Exorcist*." I looked for a grin but didn't see one.

"Okay," he said. "Then you watch your end *and* the south side. I'll watch my end *and* the north side."

That left each of us with ninety degrees of responsibility.

"Deal," I said.

The field was five acres of sunflower, millet, and doves-o-plenty. One side was bordered by a row of oaks and hackberries. The other boundary was a plot of unharvested corn. The field itself was cut into a patchwork. Some squares were newly plowed and seeded. Others were mature sections of grain, some cut and some still standing.

I knew our chances of success were slim. But what the hell, I was here. I was under the blue autumn sky with a shotgun in my hands. I walked to the other end, then looked back. Winton gave me a little wave. I gave him thumbs up. Then he turned his stool to face the other end of the field. I judged what I considered to be about forty yards from my edge and set up my gear out near the middle, my back to him. He was right in one respect. From out here, I'd at least be able to see the little buggers coming. I opened my little Ansley Fox 20, and dropped in a couple of low brass 7 1/2s.

"Tree line!" Winton called out.

I looked around and saw two birds buzzing the treetops. They were headed dead east and wouldn't be coming anywhere near me. Maybe Winton was excited. Or perhaps he only meant to cement our agreement. I settled back, took a swig from my water jug, and waited. The sun topped the canopy and hit me square in the face. September 2 would be no cooler than September 1. I pulled the little polarized clip-ons out of my shirt pocket and attached them to my glasses. The world was suddenly several shades darker, and maybe a degree cooler. But when I leaned forward from my chair, I found that my shirt was already wet and stuck to my back.

A shotgun pop brought me to attention. I turned around and saw a bird flutter down above Winton.

Then he stood up and mounted his shotgun again as the second of the pair went into evasive maneuvers. I heard the report, but the bird sped on. It streaked down the middle of the field toward me like a toy rocket.

"Bird!" he called out dutifully.

I didn't have time to think it over. The dove was on me immediately.

Swinging hard on it, I watched my front bead go past it and jerked the trigger instinctively. Nothing. So much for my instincts at 7:45 a.m.

I had hunted this field for a lot of years. I knew that no two shoots were exactly the same. The doves changed their flight patterns according to which crops were where and which food plots had fresh seed. But one thing remained constant, the northeast corner. It was a perennial entrance. The tall oaks and naked old elms that lined the river there seemed to always mark the doves' front door. But it was not an easy spot to shoot. A clump of scrawny head-tall cedars provided some cover, but they were situated close under the edge of the big trees. Birds, coming over the top, appeared out of nowhere and were often gone before you could get your gun mounted. It took quick reflexes. Yesterday, some early arrival staked out the spot and set up his gear.

He was obviously someone's guest who didn't know any better. Doves shot over the trees above him all afternoon. The poor man hardly mussed a feather. To make matters worse, the entire field looked on. It was as if we were all in the bleachers, and he was at bat for three hours. Some, I suppose, felt sorry for him. Others were wishing he'd get the hell out of there and give them that corner. Finally he did turn it over. He walked away mumbling.

A single dove cleared the trees and came floating toward me. He was in no hurry, motoring along at a sensible pace like a crop duster looking for a place to land. *This is the kind of shot I usually foul up,* I thought. When I could no longer stand it, I stood up and mounted my gun. Too soon. He veered off to the right as if I'd waved a warning flag. I suppose I had. Two opportunities, two screwups. When I looked around to see if Winton had been watching, he was staring dutifully at his assigned patch of sky. Good. I sat down, hoping I'd get another opportunity.

I'd seen other men reach Winton's age. They all seemed to respond to it in a similar way. They began to pare down a bit, eliminate some of the fluff. I suppose we all realize at some point that life indeed has an ending. Then we've got to decide how we're going to spend what's left of it. It appeared that Winton had worked out his priorities. Sitting on the front porch of the clubhouse until one or two in the morning, sipping bourbon, and retelling old jokes hadn't made the cut. I hadn't seen him participate in years. But then there's the other kind of old man, the kind who won't accept the inevitability of aging. You've seen them. They go tearing around at seventy trying to prove they can still do everything they did at fifty. I was once paired in a tennis tournament with an old fossil who spent the entire weekend strutting about in front of the young ladies with his stomach held in. When my time comes, I hope I have better sense.

A shot from Winton's spot brought me to attention. I turned around just in time to see a dove auger into the wheat stubble. Then a second one blew up in a gust of feathers overhead. A double. The old man was on his game. The remaining two birds came soaring through the field at me like a pair of fighter jets.

"Coming at you!" Winton shouted.

I didn't move a muscle. I wasn't going to spook these two. When they were right on top of me, I pulled my barrels out past the lead bird and felt the recoil of the gun. He folded up as neatly as an umbrella. I swung wildly after the second one but couldn't get a decent angle on him. He escaped over the trees like a thief. Then two more came out of the northeast corner. I froze in a half-crouched position and stuffed in two more shells. They came by juking and dodging. They'd seen me. But once past, one of them straightened out his trajectory. I aimed at his hind end and brought him down. The second one winged its way down the field toward Winton.

"Bird!" I yelled.

He was as still as a rock. But when the dove got near him, it turned hard to the right. If it hadn't seen him, it had at least been spooked by the unnatural feature in the stubble. He swung hard right to left. The dove tumbled into the short grass behind him. He was still sitting. After a long pause, he got up, walked out, and picked up the dove, taking his time, as slow as molasses. When he got back to his stool, he waved his hat in the air. Then he bent over and started packing up his gear. He'd had enough. *Well, me too, I guess.* I folded my stool and unloaded my shotgun. Winton was waiting for me at the edge of the field. When I reached him, he fell in beside me and we walked out together.

"I counted five birds for you," I said.

"That's right."

"You were hot this morning."

"Oh no. Just lucky."

"How did you do yesterday?" I asked.

"Well, I was fortunate enough to get a good spot," he said. "I shot twelve."

"Twelve yesterday and five today. That's a dove dinner."

"Yes. My wife and I do enjoy them."

Then we walked a ways farther without speaking. The sun had a good angle in the sky now, and the temperature was climbing. I could see Pinky and the Deacon waiting for us at the top of the levee, tiny sunlit figures, coffee cups in hand. We stopped for a moment as Winton busied himself with his gear. Maybe he wanted an excuse to rest. I took off my straw hat and fanned the top of my head.

"You left early yesterday, right after the hunt," I said.

"Yes."

"You missed a hell of a party last night."

He thought this over for a moment.

"Yes, I suppose I did," he said.

12

The Liars Room

At the Old River Rod and Gun, Bloody Mary Society and Gentlemen's Club we hadn't taken in a new member in years. So when young Dennis Newman joined the Old River, it was quite an event. He had been a guest at the club on a few occasions, so he was somewhat familiar with the property. But as far as the fellows, I'm afraid it took him a while to adjust. Anyone joining a new organization must learn the customs and traditions of the place. At the Old River we had developed, over the years, certain ways of looking at things. To some people they may appear odd.

Opening day of duck season that year was an unusually cold one for early December. A stiff north wind was even pushing a few snowflakes around. So the prospects for success looked good. Most of the fellows were present.

"I believe I'd better take the new man out with me this morning," Deacon Maxwell announced.

"Why is that, Deacon?" I asked.

"Because with me he's most likely to experience a good duck hunt, and after all, it is his first official day as a member."

"But why do you think you ...?"

"Okay, if I have to spell it out for you, I'm talking about waterfowling skills, my friend, and in particular calling ducks. We wouldn't want the young man to come back empty handed on his very first hunt, would we?"

By 9:30 that morning, Brother Harley Phipps and I had two mallards and two teal on our strap and were ready for breakfast. Brother Harley insisted that we thank the Almighty for our success before leaving the blind. I allowed him to speak for both of us. On our way back from the field, we ran into our new member behind the lodge.

"Good morning, Dennis," I said.

"Good morning, Mr. Bob," he answered. In the South it is customary for a young man to address an older one in that way. When I first began to experience this in my early sixties, I didn't like it. I'm long past protesting now.

"How was your hunt?" I asked.

"I'm sorry to say it didn't go very well."

"Oh?"

"Mr. Maxwell called all morning, but the ducks wouldn't come in. We moved the decoys around a couple of times, but it didn't help. He tried every duck call he had."

That evening Spoony Odom, our excellent camp cook, prepared duck gumbo with mushrooms and okra. It was a special evening, and we did everything we could to make young Newman feel welcome. After we'd had a dessert of rice pudding, those of us who didn't have kitchen duty began trailing off to the TV room.

When the lodge still functioned as a proper farmhouse many decades ago, the TV room was the family parlor. These days, the room's high ceiling, old waterfowling pictures, and ancient fireplace have an odd effect on some people. Sometimes duck hunters are prone to embellish and exaggerate events, oftentimes beyond recognition. The TV rarely gets turned on.

"I've got a cigar here that's calling my name," Roach Patton said as he pulled the cellophane off a corona. Marvin J. Beagle, attorney-at-law, poured himself a last finger of scotch.

"Deacon, we haven't heard from you yet," Marvin J. said. The Deacon had been uncharacteristically quiet during dinner. "How did you and our new man make out this morning?"

The Deacon got to his feet. "If I may, first let me officially welcome Mr. Dennis Newman into our fold," he said with much decorum. "He is a fine gentleman and a good sportsman, and I feel that he will be a great asset here at the Old River. I look forward to many years of fellowship and ..."

"I hear you two got skunked," Pinky Lipman said.

"Well, I wouldn't quite say ..." the Deacon began, turning slightly red faced.

"I saw plenty of ducks over your way," Pinky continued. "Couldn't you call them in?"

"Well, now I'll tell you, Pink," the Deacon replied. "What happened was ... you see, uh ... Listen, you fellows know I'm a pretty darn good with a duck call. But this morning those ducks wouldn't respond to anything. Finally, as we were packing up to leave, I happened to look behind us and I think I saw a ... uh ... a danged red fox running through the weeds! Well, I'm convinced that varmint was crouched out there near our decoys all morning, and those ducks could see him. Of course that kept them from coming anywhere near our spread!"

"Well, I'll be damned," Pogo Walters said.

"A fox, imagine that!" Spoony added.

Young Newman stared at the Deacon with a puzzled look. Then he searched the other faces around the room as if anticipating some explanation. None came.

"Yep, a fox. That explains the whole thing," the Deacon reiterated.

The next weekend Captain Anderson insisted on hunting with our new member. The Captain is retired Navy and a former engineering officer. He enjoys young people since they give him an opportunity to lecture on various subjects that interest him. He's a whiz with mechanical things and likes to use terms most people are unfamiliar with like thrum, rooster valve, and gob bearing. After the hunt, I encountered young Newman on the back porch as he was getting out of his waders and inquired about his morning.

"Well, we got three," he answered. "I had a little trouble with my shotgun. An empty hung in the action. Captain Anderson popped it out with a little tool."

That evening, when it was the Captain's time to speak, he turned his backside to the fire and addressed the room. "May I first say that our newest member is an upright lad," he boomed. "I will go to sea ... I mean the field with him anytime."

"How'd you do?" Pinky asked.

"Fine, fine," the Captain assured him. Then he continued. "We might have done better, but unfortunately, my young mate had some issues with his autoloader."

"Yes, there was a ..." young Newman began.

"I, however, was able to disassemble the piece in the duck blind and make some intricate adjustments," the Captain interrupted. "We've got it clicking like a rooster valve now, don't we, son?"

Several of the members nodded their approval. "Good for you, Cap!" Brother Harley Phipps said. Newman's jaw dropped slightly, and he looked at the Captain with a baffled expression.

As the season wore on, the hunting prospects worsened and then picked up again. Large numbers of ducks finally arrived on the big refuge and began foraging in neighboring river bottoms. One weekend Newman was teamed with Pogo Walters. After the hunt, I fell in with a group that was leaving the field. "Morning, Mr. Bob," our new member said, addressing me.

"Good morning, Dennis," I said. "I trust you had a good hunt."

"We bagged a couple. Mr. Walters shot a nice pintail, and that old dog of his made a pretty good retrieve." Then he slowed his walk to put some distance between us and the others. "Listen, Mr. Bob, there's something I've been wanting to ask you about," he said. "Maybe you can ..."

"Come on, Newman, if you're going to the café with the rest of us, you'd better not lag behind," Roach shouted. "There's a stack of pancakes over there calling my name."

That evening in the TV room, Pogo's old gray-muzzled Labrador retriever, Gladys, lay fast asleep in front of the fire. "How old is Gladys now?" the Deacon inquired.

"Well, I guess she's about ... I forget. But she's getting on."

"How'd she do this morning?"

"Oh, fine. I winged a big pintail this morning, and she ..." Then Pogo paused and allowed his eyes to wander around the room. His gaze went from one old waterfowling print to another. He saw the vast marshes, the flooded timber, the celebrated old clubs, the noble dogs and hunters frozen in time, and when he spoke again, his voice sounded softer and more distant. "I suppose that bird went down a mile away," he continued, looking back into the fire.

"Well, I said to myself, 'we'll never find that one. That duck is lost for sure.' But you know, old Gladys saw that bird go down too. So just on a hunch, I slid back the top on the dog box and told her to 'go.' Now, for your ordinary dog, that would've been an impossible retrieve considering he'd have to swim the slough, cross that big field, and finally go into the woods after the mark. But sure enough, a half hour later here comes old Gladys as pretty as you please with that big sprig in her mouth. You've never seen anything like it!"

"Gladys is quite a dog, Po," the Deacon said.

"Yes, sir, you got yourself a legend there," Roach added.

With this, young Newman looked at Pogo and then at each of us with an expression of utter bewilderment.

I finally had an opportunity to hunt with our new member on the very last weekend. We got a late start that morning so by the time we were in our blind with our gear put away, it was already shooting time. "Mr. Bob, I'm really glad we got to hunt together today," he said. "There's something I'd like to talk ..."

"Ducks, son! Your end!" I interrupted. Several mallards were trying to come into the east side of our spread and working against a very strong wind. Dennis quickly shouldered his auto. He fired and then after a moment fired twice more. The birds turned and slipped quickly downwind. Afterward, he tried to be upbeat and flippant about that first set of misses. But things got worse. The wind blew very hard all morning, and my hunting partner was on the downwind side so he got all the shooting. I didn't dare attempt a shot since the muzzles of my shotgun would have been much too close to his ear. I try to be aware of such things, having lost a portion of my hearing to overzealous companions through the years. The thing is, he didn't hit a bird the whole time. I was sympathetic. Wind can be a tricky thing, and we all have poor days when it comes to wing shooting. But I decided it was best that I not say anything. On the walk back to the lodge, he was noticeably quiet.

That evening in the TV room Brother Harley asked me, "how'd you fellows fare this morning? I hope the Lord blessed you with a good hunt."

"I..., I'll defer to my companion, "I said, concerned that I might say the wrong thing.

"I hear you struck out," Pinky said, addressing Newman.

"Well, you could say ..." Newman began.

"I saw a lot of birds working your spread. What happened?"

"What happened was I, we ..."

"I heard quite a bit of shooting over your way too," Pinky continued.

I could see my hunting partner's mind searching for some answer that might salvage his dignity, some nuance, some parsing of speech that would put an acceptable spin on things. Apparently he found none.

"Well ... you see, of course ... what happened was we, uh ..." he stammered. Then in desperation he blurted out, "We didn't have a dog!"

"I know, but did you ...?"

"We didn't have a dog!" he repeated.

"So you're saying you lost some birds?"

He paused a moment to think this over, then continued. "Yeah, that's it, we lost some ducks! We lost some ducks in the corn because we didn't have a dog!" Then his voice got a little stronger as he appeared to gain confidence. "I hope one of you fellows with a dog will get out there first light and pick those up." Then after a moment he added, "Of course by then a hawk will probably have claimed them, and there won't even be a feather." He looked at me with a pleading expression. I didn't say a word.

"Fellas," Roach said, "I think I hear that red wine calling my name. I believe I'll have another little glass."

Someone started in retelling an old tale that always got belly laughs. I glanced over at young Dennis Newman. He was leaning far back on the sofa, staring into the flickering flames with a self-satisfied smile.

13

An Impeccable Pedigree

"You know, Pinky," the Deacon said, "sometimes a man must admit to himself that he owns a dog that won't hunt."

"What do you mean by that?" Pinky asked, obviously offended.

"Well, some dogs just don't take to it," the Deacon replied. He was watching Pinky Lipman's yellow Lab lying on the floor of the duck blind lazily licking his front paws. The Deacon and I had joined Pinky that morning at the Old River Rod and Gun, Bloody Mary Society and Gentlemen's Club to hunt ducks. Unfortunately, we had been impelled to pick up all three of our birds by hand. Pinky's dog showed no inclination whatever to retrieve them.

"You're wrong, Deacon!" Pinky countered. "Prince is young yet. He'll come around."

"It just seems to me," the Deacon continued, "you've put in a lot of time and effort ..."

"Listen, my friend," Pinky interrupted, "this dog has a pedigree that's out of this world."

"Maybe so, but ..."

"He's from the finest bloodlines in the country. There's not one name in his lineage that's not a champion. Why, his grandma was Mother Hubbard's Tea Set! I'm sure you've heard of her!"

"No, I can't say I ..."

"Well, you take it from me, she was a great one, and her blood is running through Prince's veins. Sooner or later he's going to blossom. Have I shown you his papers?"

"I believe you did."

Pinky had purchased Daddy Warbucks Golden Prince of Paducah as a pup from a very reputable breeder and had paid a dear price for him. When the dog was the proper age, he delivered him to the finest retriever trainer in the region. Two days later, the trainer called and asked Pinky to pick up his dog. He explained that Prince had shown no interest at all in retrieving, was not in the least bit attracted to bird scent, and seemed to have an aversion to water. Pinky responded with indignation and resolved to train the dog himself. He promptly went out and bought two thousand dollars' worth of equipment. I asked him several times in the ensuing months how Prince's training was coming along. He was invariably vague.

"Deacon, you've disliked Prince from the beginning," Pinky continued. "You've never said one nice thing about him."

"It's not that I *dislike* him. Anyway, I'm sure he's a fine pet."

"Pet?"

"Yes, I just thought that since he ..."

"I didn't pay all that money for a pet. Believe me, one of these days he's going to be a great waterfowling dog. Then you'll be eating your words, you and all the fellows. But since you asked, no he's not much of a pet. Doesn't like the kids. You'd think they smelled like cat pee or something. Hell, maybe they do!"

"The wife then?"

"She's a parakeet person."

At the Old River, it seemed there were always too few dogs to go around. The Deacon and I and most of the other older members had long outlived our various Jacks, Beaus, Belles, and Busters. And fetching one's own birds in a flooded cornfield with a foot of soft mud on the bottom is no easy task. So, the two of us were always eager to team up with a dog owner. Unfortunately, some of the dogs were better than others.

A few weeks later, on a balmy afternoon when there was scant hope of ducks flying, we again found ourselves in Pinky's company. Since there was little use in going to the field, he decided to take Prince out on the boat dock and work on his water retrieves. Some comfy lawn chairs were out there so the Deacon and I settled in to look on.

"I've got an idea, fellows," Pinky said. "This isn't in any of the books. But with a dog like Prince I figure you've got to be creative. He's not your ordinary backyard retriever, you know. He's high strung. After all, his daddy was Uncle Wiggles Cha Cha Cha." He told Prince to sit, then went to his pickup topper and brought back two standard canvas training dummies, a bucket, and a greasy paper bag. "We're about to make a breakthrough here," he said. He reached into the bag and pulled out what appeared to be a pork chop.

"What's that, Pink?" the Deacon asked.

"It's a damn pork chop! Haven't you ever seen a pork chop?"

"Yes, I just never saw anyone train a ..."

"Like I said, this isn't in any of the books." Pinky waved the pork chop under Prince's nose, who made a half-hearted attempt to snatch it. But Pinky jerked it away. "Aha! You want that, don't you?" he purred in a soft voice. "Smells good, huh?" A drop of saliva dripped off Prince's chin. Pinky fished a piece of string out of his pocket, tied the two dummies together, and then tied the pork chop securely on top. He tossed the dummies with pork chop attached a short distance off the dock.

"All right," he said. "Go get it, boy!" Prince looked at Pinky, then back at the pork chop. "Go on, I said. Get in there!" Prince didn't budge.

"Okay. So, it's that water thing then," Pinky concluded. He lowered the bucket into the lake, filled it to the top, dipped his fingers in, and carefully sprinkled a little water on the dog's nose. "See, it's only water!" he said reassuringly. Pinky dribbled a little more down Prince's back. He didn't seem to mind. I was beginning to think Pinky was getting somewhere. Then he dumped the remaining contents of the bucket on the dog's head. Suddenly, Prince let out a terrified howl and bolted. Shocked and surprised, Pinky stumbled backward to the edge of the dock. He teetered there for a moment, flapping his arms like a fledgling sparrow as if he hoped to propel himself forward enough to regain his balance. Ultimately, he lost the contest and went backward into the lake. When he stood up in the waist-deep water, Prince was hightailing it across a distant field. "Prince, wait!" he called out, "Look!" He cupped his hands and began splashing water onto his face and chest. "Look, it's only water! Priiiiiiiiiince!"

One cold Saturday morning toward the end of the season, the Deacon and I were happy to have the opportunity to hunt with Pogo Walters. Pogo owned a very serviceable old retriever named Gladys. Just as the three of us were about to start for the field, Pinky arrived. "Which pit are you fellows going to hunt this morning?" he asked. The Deacon told him. "Hey, that one's got a dog box on both ends! Mind if Prince and I tag along?"

"Well ... all right," the Deacon said.

"You see, I've been thinking," Pinky continued. "I believe if Prince could watch Gladys work once or twice, he might, you know, he just might get it. That light in his head might switch on."

When we walked into the bottom, several hundred ducks took flight. It was too dark to identify the species, but they appeared to be a mixed flock, possibly mallards and widgeons.

The Deacon assigned Pogo and Gladys to the left end since it was downwind and likely to see the most action. Pinky and Prince took the position on the right. The weather was cold and blustery that morning, which gave us hope that some of those birds might just come back. Prince soon curled up in his dog box and began licking his paws.

"Why does he do that?" the Deacon asked.

"I suppose it's because he's a pure-bred." Pinky said.

"What do you mean?"

"I believe pure-bred dogs are more particular about things like personal hygiene."

"But he's a dog."

"So?"

Pinky soon thought better of that and got Prince into a sitting position. "All right, boy," he coaxed. "Watch Gladys, okay?" When the sun was just about to peep above the horizon, a half-dozen mallards appeared over the river. The Deacon gave them a highball, and the lead hen tipped her wings in our direction. They made a wide turn, circled behind us, then looped out front again. As they made pass after pass, the Deacon softened his call until he was down to a whiney squawk. I looked to my left and saw Gladys watching the birds fixedly, her eyes round with excitement. When the flock made a low sweep over the decoys, she trembled in anticipation. I gazed down at Pinky's end and noticed that Prince's head was no longer visible above the edge of his dog box. Then I heard a slurping sound.

The ducks made a final turn and started back toward us. Finally, when they were poised over our spread, the Deacon shouted, "Get 'em!" and we rolled back the top. I was first on my feet and took the surest shot, a green head directly out front. I saw the Deacon take a duck on my right. Pogo hit a widgeon on his end but not solidly. The bird fell a good distance out, deep into the flooded corn and obscured from view. But I didn't doubt for a moment that Gladys had marked it.

"How many, boys?" the Deacon barked.

"I count three," I answered.

"We better get mine first, Deacon," Pogo said.

"Send her, Po!"

Pogo unhooked Gladys's tether and shouted, "Back!" She bolted out of her box, raced across the narrow strip of ground in front of the pit, and charged into the water.

"Look, Prince! See what Gladys is doing?" Pinky said. "She's swimming out to find that duck. No, no Prince, over here!" He grasped the dog's head with both hands and pointed it in the proper direction. Gladys disappeared into the cornstalks. A few minutes later she reappeared, paddling steadily toward the pit with the widgeon in her mouth. "Now, watch Gladys, Prince!" Pinky said. He held the dog's head and moved it to follow Gladys's progress as if it were a movie camera. "Attaboy! Take it all in!" When Gladys delivered the widgeon to Pogo, he next sent her for the Deacon's bird, which was farthest out of the remaining two. Finally, she brought in the third duck. All three retrieves were flawless.

"Did I ever tell you fellows that Prince's granddaddy was Mr. Ed's Eenie, Meenie, Miney, Moe?" Pinky asked.

"I believe you did."

An hour later a group of late season green-winged teal buzzed us. We quickly got down and covered up. When they made another pass, we were late rolling back the top, but I managed to swing hard on the last bird and connect. It fell on dry land not twenty yards behind the pit.

Just as Pogo was about to send Gladys, Pinky stopped him. "Wait!" he said. "Let's let Prince get this one." He climbed out of the pit, coaxed the dog out of his box, then led him to where the bird had fallen. "Sit!" he said. Then he gently pried Prince's jaws apart and placed the little duck in his mouth. "Stay!" Pinky ordered. Then he began backing away, stopping every few steps to repeat the command. Finally, he resumed his position in the pit. "Okay, fellows," he whispered, "Nobody move." Meanwhile, Prince seemed to be fixated on a formation of passing clouds, having apparently forgotten that he had the teal in his mouth. "Oh, Prince!" Pinky called, "over here, boy. Look!" The

ISTOCK

dog gazed quizzically at Pinky, as if he thought he might be in possession of another pork chop. Then very cautiously Pinky said, "Okay ... come." Prince didn't budge. "Here, boy," Pinky coaxed. The dog searched each of our faces with a look of bewilderment. "You can do it, come," Pinky pleaded. Then he began a little two-note singsong that went, "Here, boy, here, boy, here, boy." Finally, the dog acknowledged Pinky's entreaty and took a tentative step forward with the teal still in his mouth. "That's it! Come on! That's the stuff! Here, boy, here, boy."

At last he began to take slow, hesitant steps toward his master. "Look at that!" Pinky shouted. "Isn't that magnificent?! Didn't I tell you Prince would come around! Isn't that beautiful?" Somebody get a camera! Who's got a camera?"

14

The Senior Duck Hunt

At the Old River Rod and Gun, Bloody Mary Society and Gentlemen's Club, the age of the average member was trending down. Every time one of the old fellows passed away or dropped out due to infirmity, he was replaced by a younger man. So a new generation was supplanting the old right before our eyes. Still, Deacon Maxwell and I and a couple of others held on. After all, we had decades invested in the place: decades of amateur carpentry, frozen water pipes, battles with beavers and muskrats, floods, droughts, and unpredictable duck seasons.

Don't misunderstand me. I have no animosity toward our young members. These fellows have made some fine improvements. Not only have they upgraded the food crops and water structures and as a result, the duck hunting, they've outfitted the lodge with central heat and air and a flat screen TV. Furthermore, we now have a second bathroom for the ladies. When I say ladies, I mean the wives and daughters of the younger men. It turns out, these fellows bring their families down during the warm months for camping and fishing. And according to the club log, several wives and sweethearts even hunted ducks last year. We older men find this curious. You see, our generation used the club to more or less get away from our families. For us it was a place where a man could stay up late and smoke a cigar.

And so it was on the third weekend of the season we, the last four old members, gathered for our annual duck hunt. The young fellows had again graciously granted us sole use of old No. 7 duck blind. In attendance were Deacon Maxwell, Brother Harley Phipps, Pogo Walters, and me, Ranger Bob McDill. That's what they all call me, Ranger Bob or Ranger. Barring weekdays, we were limited to a Saturday hunt since Brother Harley Phipps never misses Sunday church services, morning and evening.

The Deacon, as always, arrived a day early. The rest of us joined him the following morning at 5:30 a.m., for coffee and biscuits at the kitchen table. As meager a meal as it was, Brother Harley insisted on saying a lengthy grace. After a time, I could see the Deacon was getting antsy. The moment Harley finished giving thanks, he blurted out, "There's a load of ducks in the bottom, boys! I saw them pouring in last night just after sundown!" Apparently, he had held this news until we were all seated and properly attentive. Sure enough, the group perked right up.

"That's great news, Deacon!" I said. "What kind of ducks?"

"Huh?"

"What kind of ducks?" I repeated in a louder voice.

"What?" he asked, cupping his hand to his ear.

"WHAT KIND OF DUCKS?" I shouted.

"Big ducks, Ranger, mostly mallards!"

"Why aren't you wearing your hearing aid, Deacon?"

"Huh?"

"YOUR HEARING AID?"

"Oh, somebody stole it."

"Who'd steal a hearing aid?"

"There are many hearing-impaired people in this country, my friend."

The Deacon was always the most eager to get to the field and therefore the first to suit up. After he'd downed several biscuits with butter and grape jelly, he disappeared into the bunk room, returning a few minutes later in full regalia: chest-high insulated waders, camo foul-weather coat with hood, and big down mittens. From one lanyard around his neck hung every waterfowl call imaginable. Strung on the other were probably a hundred trophy leg bands. "Let's head for the field, boys," he said. "You can't get on the train if you're not at the station!" It was his favorite metaphor.

So we trekked down the main levee before dawn and crossed the field of corn stubble between there and old No. 7. I carried the Deacon's robotic duck and his seat cushion as well as my own gear while Pogo lugged the Deacon's extra ammo and bag of toiletries. The Deacon himself managed the rest of his things. He believed in being prepared for any need that might arise in the field … even though the lodge was a ten-minute walk away. None of us felt it was worth the trouble of argument. Unburdened of half his gear, the Deacon got off to a healthy lead, loping along twenty yards ahead of us. Pogo and I felt it was our duty to hang back with Harley, who was making his way pretty slowly. In the darkness I could make out two other parties of hunters on the levee behind us. They were young fellows and appeared to be headed for No. 8 and No. 9.

The seniors had not been very successful on our annual hunt the last few years. Lately, when everyone gathered at the lodge after the morning's shoot, the young fellows had been showing up with impressive strings of ducks. We had little more to show than a skinny gadwall or two. This embarrassed the Deacon terribly. To him, such a shabby performance not only reflected poorly on the old members but was an indictment of his leadership and ability to blow a duck call.

The old wooden duck blind at No. 7 had recently been replaced with a steel pit. The young fellows claim it's easier to camouflage since it only sticks up about eighteen inches above the mud. I suppose that's true. But shooting out of it has taken some getting used to.

"I'll take the right end," the Deacon announced, lighting the interior with his flashlight. "Ranger Bob, you take the left end." We usually deferred to the Deacon's judgment when duck hunting since he put in more hours at it than probably anyone else living. "Brother Harley, step down in there and take the spot next to me," he said.

"Honestly, Maxwell, I'd rather not sit next to you," Harley replied.

"Why not?"

"You've got more gear than L. L. Bean. I'll be scrunched up in that tiny little space, and my bad hip will start bothering me."

"Suit yourself," the Deacon grumbled.

After we had all answered the call of nature for the second time in the last half hour, we took our positions. I had the left end, and Brother Harley, who spent an interminable amount of time getting down into the pit, took the spot on my right. The top, which rolls back for shooting, is a two-piece affair. So Harley and I were to work our top while the Deacon and Pogo would deal with theirs.

"Five minutes till shooting time," the Deacon declared, looking at his watch, "the longest five minutes in a man's life!" After fussing with his gear and checking the time a dozen more times, he announced, "we're legal!"

"I've got another minute and a half on my watch," Harley said.

"Load 'em up, fellows, and close the top" the Deacon ordered, who either hadn't heard Harley or was simply ignoring him. "You can't get on the train if you're not ..." Just then six ducks appeared downwind, stopping him in midsentence. They saw our decoys and made a wide circle. The Deacon gave them a little descending four-note request, then another. Then he offered a more insistent call, five notes with the first one elongated. The lead duck turned.

"I don't see them," Pogo said, adjusting his glasses. The birds circled widely behind us. Then they made another sweep out front. "I still don't see them," Pogo said. "Do you see them, Harley?" After what seemed like eternity, they sailed in.

"Let's get 'em!" the Deacon yelled as he began struggling to push back the top on his end. Harley and I rolled ours back with some difficulty, and I got to my feet. However, when I tried to shoulder my shotgun, the stock caught on my coat. By the time I got off a shot, it was wasted on an out-of-range bird. *That wouldn't have happened ten years ago*, I thought. When it was over, we had put only one duck on the water. It appeared we might once again be in for some embarrassment.

"How many did we get?" the Deacon called out.

"Just one," Harley shouted.

"What?"

"ONE!"

"Humph, one," the Deacon grumbled.

We had all long outlived our dogs, and without a young person in the party, we had no choice but to fetch our own birds. No one else was showing any eagerness to go after our duck, so I volunteered. But when I waded in, I found the water to be much colder than I remembered it being in years past and almost to the top of my waders. There were also several inches of muck on the bottom, which made each step difficult. When I got back to the pit, I was out of breath.

"I'm not looking forward to my turn, fellas," Harley said. "Walking in that mud is hard on my bad knee."

"I thought you had a bad hip," I said.

"I do," he answered. "And that's the reason for my bad foot. I'm not complaining, mind you, but you see with a bad hip and a bad knee, the body weight is often improperly applied which can lead to ..."

"Ducks!" the Deacon interrupted. This turned out to be three wood ducks headed for the flooded willows at the other end of our property. By the time he sorted through his inventory and found a "woody" call, they were out of sight.

Then we sat for a long period without seeing a thing. The canopy had cleared, and it was starting to look like one of those cold blue days when ducks raft up on the big water in the refuge, and hunters are left watching fluffy white clouds float by. But one had to admit it was all quite lovely.

"What a magnificent morning!" Harley gushed. "Every day I thank the Lord for giving me another day on this beautiful earth."

"So, you talk to the Lord quite a bit?" the Deacon asked.

"I try to *always* be in fellowship with the Almighty."

"While you're at it this morning, why don't you ask Him to send a few ducks our way?"

"I don't bother the Lord with trivial matters, Maxwell."

Harley always addressed the Deacon as Maxwell rather than Deacon Maxwell or Deacon since he didn't hold the Presbyterian Church in high regard.

"Trivial!?" the Deacon responded.

About that time Pogo said he needed another nature break, so we all four climbed out of the pit. It was rare that when one of us called for one, we didn't all take advantage of the opportunity. Then the Deacon said we'd best get back in the pit and close the top since you can't get on the train if you're not at the station. After spending an hour without seeing a bird, someone suggested we adjourn to the lodge for a proper breakfast. Just as we were about to start packing our gear, a dozen ducks appeared overhead. The Deacon put up a little soft quacking and chuckling so as not to spook them. I nudged the jerk string carefully to lay some ripples on the water.

"I don't see them," Pogo said. They lifted higher and banked over the river.

"Harley, do you see them? I don't see them."

When they turned back, they made a wide circle. I put in my ear-

ISTOCK

plugs in anticipation. One more loop, and they headed into our spread. I had a moment earlier shed my coat, and my finger was resting on the safety of my old auto. There's nothing like a second chance.

"Get 'em!" the Deacon hollered.

I was determined to respect Harley's space, so I limited myself to the two ducks off my end of the pit. I nailed the first one just at the edge of the flooded corn. The other sailed over the top. I covered it up with my front sight, pulled the trigger, and saw it plop into the dry field behind us. Meanwhile my partners had been banging away. I turned back just in time to see Harley take a last duck out front. Then there was a long silence. I counted the downed birds.

"How many?" the Deacon called out.

"I see seven," I answered.

"Huh?" He was now standing on his ammo box to get a better view.

"Seven!" I hollered. "SEVEN!"

"No, no, you're wrong, Ranger. There's seven!" he shouted.

We had bagged four green heads and three drake widgeons. No one had shot a hen. It was damn near perfect. I looked down at the Deacon's end of the pit and saw a single tear of joy glistening on his cheek. Then I noticed he wasn't wearing his earplugs.

"Deacon, you're not wearing your earplugs!"

"What?"

"You're not wearing your earplugs!"

"What?"

"YOU'RE NOT WEARING EARPLUGS!"

"I know, Ranger. I really should use the little buggers. But the problem is, I don't hear worth a damn when I'm wearing earplugs." Harley guffawed at this, then checked himself and cleared his throat. The Deacon, of course, hadn't heard him. A breeze picked up about that time, and our decoys began bobbing gently against their tethers.

"Okay, who's ready for a comfort break?" Pogo asked.

PART TWO

Farther Afield

15

Going Mental

From *Shooting Sportsman*

I was at the right end in a line of eight guns. We stood in ankle-deep grass at the bottom of a long sloping hill, looking to the top where the birds were beginning to take flight ahead of the beaters. There were not many pheasants. Those that came, came slowly and deliberately, beating their wings hard to gain enough altitude to make the tree line behind us. It seemed to take them forever to get to the line of guns. I had ample time to think while watching the first bird come toward me; plenty of time to rehearse the shot, change my stance, and adjust my glasses, as it turns out, too much time. I not only missed the first bird, I missed the second. Then I was really in trouble.

"What am I doing, Brian?" I asked my loader.

"You're not following through, sir," he answered. Brian Robinson was the veteran of hundreds of drives. He was a rosy-cheeked Yorkshireman, who knew shooting and knew his terrain. If anyone could see bad form, it was Brian.

I winged one bird, then missed another.

"What is it, Brian? Help me," I pleaded.

"You're pointing, sir. You're not flowing."

Soon I couldn't have hit the wall with a handful of beans. It had happened again. Just let me get off to a bad start and then start trying to correct my mistakes. Soon I'm adjusting my swing, changing my stance, and swearing that on the next shot I'll do this or that differently. In no time I'm moving stiffly and mechanically and missing way too often.

When the drive was over, I could tell that Brian was unhappy with me. I've always suspected that loaders have bets riding on the outcome. There's probably a pot to be collected by the loader attached to the gun with the highest number of birds. Why else are they so disappointed when you shoot poorly and so elated when you shoot well?

I remember one Georgia quail hunt where I began by missing two shots on the first covey rise. Perhaps they were difficult shots, shots I shouldn't have taken. It didn't matter, the damage was done. On the next rise, I vowed to put my weight on my left foot. Then I resolved to be more patient and pick my shots more carefully and, of course, correct my lead. The more thinking I did, the worse it got. Soon I couldn't have hit a bull in the behind with a bass fiddle. My guide, a young man with whom I had hunted for years, saw my anger and frustration. Finally he had mercy on me.

"Are you about ready to go to the house, Mr. Bob?"

"I thought you'd never ask," I answered.

He later told me about another fellow he'd seen do the same thing. He'd shot poorly the first morning and had then worried himself into a state of depression. The more he worried, the worse he got. He finally locked himself in his room for the last two days of the hunt and had his meals put under the door.

After watching me fall apart on the skeet range one afternoon, a friend suggested I get some advice. It was the second time in a month he'd seen me choke.

"I think it's in your head, man," he said.

"My what?" I queried.

"Your head. You're wound up as tight as a tick," he said. "Maybe you ought to look into this mental stuff."

So reluctantly, I set about to explore the mysteries of the human psyche. After all, what did I have to lose? Things couldn't get any worse. I signed up for a series of lessons with famous local shooting instructor John Wiley.

"So, tell me about this problem of yours," he said.

"Well, lately I've been choking, freezing up, and when I get that way, I can't hit the ground with a shovel."

He listened carefully and suggested we start with a review of basics. After a little work on stance and swing, we moved on to more challenging targets. And sure enough, it happened. Right before his eyes, I began to tighten up. The tighter I got, the more I missed. It was then I began to hear phrases that I'd never heard before from a shooting instructor.

"Trust yourself," he said.

"Trust what?" I asked.

"Trust yourself," he answered, "trust your instincts."

"What instincts?" I said, "I don't have any instincts."

"Oh, yes you do, but you're not listening to them. You're thinking too much. You're getting in your own way," he said, "just let it happen."

I couldn't believe my ears. This man sounded like some sort of new age shaman instructing me in the paths of enlightenment. It was all so spiritual, so cosmic, so ethereal. In fact it sounded downright Eastern.

"Listen to yourself, Grasshopper."

"John," I said, "you don't sound like a shooting instructor, you sound like a bloomin' Zen master."

John denied knowing much about Zen. He had not grown up in the 1960s in America and therefore had missed the much eulogized hippie experience. What he did know about was shooting. As it turns out, that kind of teaching has been making its way into sport for years. It began with tennis, spread to golf, and is now so widespread it has a name, the Modern Sports Psychology Movement. Writers like Tim Gallwey and Dr. Robert Rotella have taught pros and amateurs alike about the "inner game." Most big-time golfers now not only employ a coach, but also a shrink, or rather, a sports psychologist.

"What you're doing is listening to your demons," John said. "You're allowing that negative voice inside you to speak. It's the voice that doubts, that tells you, you can't make this shot."

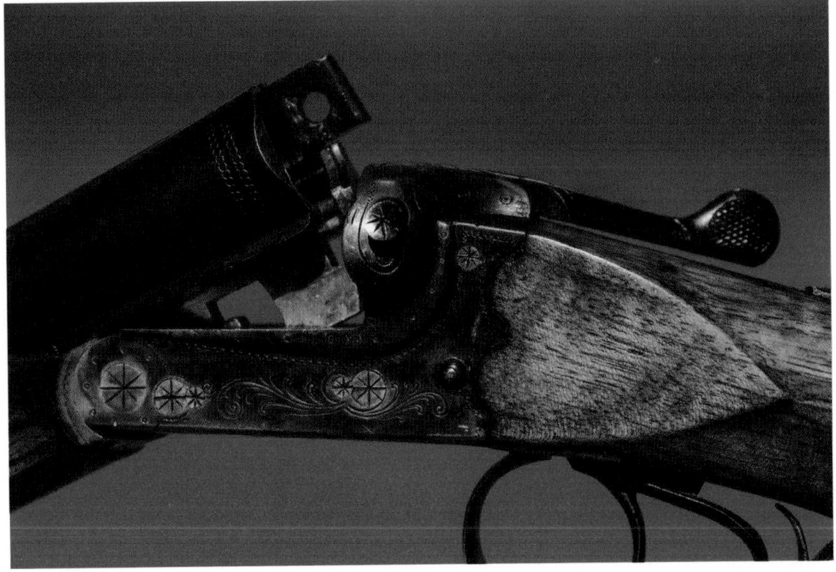

ISTOCK

"Are you accusing me of hearing voices?" I asked.

"Well, no, the voice is you. It's just the negative part of you."

"Okay I'll admit it, I've heard that voice," I said.

"If you miss a couple of shots, your negative voice makes an assessment. It says you're not shooting well today or you're not very good at this particular shot. When you listen to that voice, you allow doubt to enter your mind. Then you start trying to overcome doubt by consciously thinking about how to hit that particular target. You begin trying to calculate distance, lead, and swing. And, of course, your shooting only gets worse. The calculations are too complex. You can't do it. You should be relying on your instincts instead."

"That's easy for you to say," I countered.

"Don't think," he said, "trust your instincts."

"So which is it, stop thinking or stop doubting?" I asked.

"Look at it this way," he answered. "I think, therefore I doubt."

"That's deep," I said.

"I know it sounds silly, but the main thing is for you to stop listening to your negative voice."

"How do I do that?" I asked.

"You must separate your negative self from your real self. For some people, that's hard to do. Do you have any anger left over from childhood?"

"Well, we were the last family on the street to get a color TV," I said.

He pretended he hadn't heard me. "The best way to stop thinking is to visualize only one thing."

"What's that?" I asked.

"The target as it's breaking, how it looks and feels when you break the target."

Use the force, Luke, I thought.

"Remember this," he said. "When Mr. Doubt knocks at your door, you don't have to let him in."

John related to me what had happened to him in one particular British sporting clays tournament. He was one round away from winning the whole business but missed his final three shots.

"What happened?" I asked.

"I started thinking," he said.

But as he explained, this doesn't discount the need for practice. One can't pick up a shotgun for the first time and shoot like Colonel Bogardus simply by making one's mind go blank. It's necessary to break lots of targets from lots of angles and lots of distances. Only by doing that can you learn how hitting the target "feels" and "looks" in each situation. Or as some shooting instructors call it, "the picture." The picture is what that perfect moment looks like: the target, the distance, the lead, etc. When your instinct sees the picture, your instinct pulls the trigger.

The opposite of choking or freezing up is when you're in the flow state or the zone. We've probably all experienced that at one time or another. It's that feeling you get when everything's working. When you are unaware of other people or voices or anything else around you. There's only you and the target. You're completely focused and totally confident. It's quite exhilarating.

Dr. Mihaly Csikszentmihalyi (yes that's really his name) of the University of Chicago describes it this way: "In the flow state, action follows upon action according to an internal logic that seems to need no conscious intervention ... there is little distinction between self and environment, between stimulus and response and between past, present and future."

Sometimes circumstances come together to bring this about. If you think about it, your best shots are usually made when you're in a hurry. I know mine are. It seems the less time we have, the less likely we are to doubt ourselves and the less likely we are to consciously think about swing, lead, etc., therefore allowing instinct to do it. Thus even a mediocre shot can sometimes find himself in the flow state.

I remember one beautiful afternoon in the north of England. I drew a butt behind the line of guns in a backup position. I was not backing up the line because of my shooting ability; I simply drew that number. Brian and I were positioned in the woods in a small clearing. There was an opening in the canopy above us that couldn't have been more than forty feet across. Within that little patch of blue sky, I was expected to kill fast-moving pheasants.

As the birds started flying, I realized I could just make out each one through the leaves before it appeared in the opening. There was just enough time to swing hard and fire before it disappeared above the canopy on the other side. No time to think, doubt, fidget, or worry. There was only time for instinct. I shot better than I had in years. Brian was ecstatic. He probably won the pot.

This may explain why I can shoot driven grouse. Let me clarify that. I've never seen anyone who could really shoot driven grouse, much less me. Okay,

Lord Ripon, but I never saw him shoot. Let me say that I'm not as bad on driven grouse as one might expect considering the way I shoot, say, mourning doves. The reason is obvious. There you are, crouched in a stone butt on some Scottish or English moor. When the birds first appear, coming toward you, hugging the terrain, they look to be miles away. But in a nanosecond, they are on top of you, and it's almost too late. There is just time for a shot out front and one passing. With a decent tailwind, a grouse can approach 100 miles per hour. No time for thinking or doubting here.

This is what Mr. Churchill was all about. He's universally recognized as having pioneered "instinct shooting." However, his version of it has now come under some scrutiny. He believed that if one simply swings the barrel and follows through properly, no lead is required. Of course, that's true as long as the target is close in, but most shooting instructors now know that more distant targets require lead. This is where "the picture" enters the picture. After breaking enough targets, one's subconscious supposedly memorizes these things as part of "the picture." Once you have it, your instinct-oriented instructor is very likely to ask you to once again stop thinking.

What a strange turn of events. All our lives we were told by parents, teachers, coaches, and anyone else in authority to think.

"Use your head," they told us. "Why don't you use that brain of yours?" they asked.

"You didn't think that through, did you?" they scolded.

"If you'd only use your gray matter," they pleaded.

"Think, think, think."

We were led to believe that simply putting the old noggin in gear could solve anything. If you reasoned, measured, and planned, you could have health, wealth, and happiness, even fame and fortune. All you had to do was use your head.

Oh, but listen to them now! What a terrible prank it seems life has played on us, to be suddenly, in late middle age, told that there is something thinking will not accomplish. In fact we are actually told to stop thinking. We are informed that our subconscious or instinct is more capable in some matters than our intellect and that our rational mind only gets in the way, bringing with it self-doubt. Turn off the old noodle, disconnect the brainpan, and stand there drooling and slack jawed. Then you can shoot like a champion.

And even if one vows to stop thinking, it's not that easy. Just try it. True, as an adult, I have often been accused of not thinking. People have mistakenly observed me staring stupidly out a window on a beautiful day and assumed that my mind was completely blank. Friends, co-workers, and a lifetime of women I loved have observed me in this state and concluded that the inside of my head was totally empty. But the truth is, I *was* thinking. I was thinking about fishing or sometimes duck hunting. I have found that it's very difficult to think about nothing. Just about the time you think you've achieved it, something like fishing will pop in there.

It is six months later, and I'm back in Yorkshire. Brian and I have drawn a position in the center of a line of eight guns. We are strung out along a shallow creek. In front of us and at the top of a gentle slope is a bright green kale field where the beaters have gathered to drive the birds toward us. My new friend Paul and his loader are on my right.

When the birds first start to come, I'm surprised at how many there are. Hundreds are flying fast and high. I hit a few, miss a few, and then I find the picture. They start to fall regularly. There is no time to think now, only to swing hard and fire. I pass the empty double gun to Brian on the inside, and he passes me its loaded mate on the outside, again and again. He drops a shell and stoops to pick it up, breaking our rhythm, apologizing. Now we're back in sync. They are falling like rain. The barrels are hot. Brian is giggling, calling "oh, oh, oh," then cooing like a pigeon. Still they come. I'm in the zone, flowing. All self-doubt is gone; all thought is gone; I'm pure instinct.

Finally the flight slackens and stops. The beaters move in to collect the birds. They are everywhere.

"Tremendous shooting, sir," Brian says.

My new friend Paul walks up the line grinning, eyes large, still high on adrenaline.

"Have you ever ...?" he asks, not able to finish the sentence.

"No," I say.

But I'm not cured. I have not reached some new plateau from which I can never again fall. This does not end my checkered career as a wing shot. Just let me get a bad start, miss a few shots, start thinking, correcting things, worrying. In no time I'll be fussing with my swing, my lead, and doubting myself. Pretty soon I won't be able to hit the floor with my hat. You see, it can happen at any time. When old Mr. Doubt knocks at my door, sometimes I not only invite him in, I sit him down and offer him a drink.

16

The Natural

From *Shooting Sportsman*

"Tree line!" someone called out.

I stepped out from under the row of oaks and hackberries just in time to see two gray rockets streaking overhead. I swung the barrels, covered up the first bird, and pulled the trigger. It didn't give. I fumbled for the safety. Where in the name of Nash Buckingham was the safety? As my fingers searched the gun blindly, the two birds sailed away, untouched, over the treetops. When I looked down, I found, to my surprise, that I was holding my little A. H. Fox quail gun. Oh, yes, that second set of barrels, the ones I'd had rechoked for dove shooting. I was going to try them out today. The safety was there all right, just where it was supposed to be. But I hadn't shot the gun in years, and the little switch had escaped my thumb.

What a bonehead way to start the afternoon. I sat down on my stool and began clicking the safety on and off angrily. I wanted to kick myself.

Four more birds topped the trees at the far corner of the field. "Down the middle!" someone yelled.

Harvey Jr., the best wing shot in the field, had the corner spot behind a large hay roll. When the doves cleared the canopy, he took the first one straight overhead. Then, turning around, he banged another going away for a double. The other two zoomed down the middle of the field, veering and turning like heat-seeking missiles. When they cut right, in my direction, they seemed to gain warp speed.

"Right at you, Mr. Bob!" Harvey Jr. called out.

Before I knew it, they were on top of me. I swung past the first bird, making sure the safety was off, and pulled the trigger. My pattern trailed it by a country mile.

Okay, don't panic. There's still the second one, I thought.

I hurried frantically to catch up to it with my gun barrels as it looped skyward. But somehow I got caught with my weight on my back foot. Clumsily, I stumbled backward as I pulled the trigger. The dove raced on across the tree line like an escaping felon. It was embarrassing. Harvey Jr. had seen the whole thing.

It was shaping up into one of my bad days. When I say bad day, I mean one when I couldn't hit the side of a barn while standing inside it. One when I couldn't hit an elephant with a fire hose. I'd had them before, and I knew the symptoms. Shooting is like a roll of the dice with me. Or better yet, like a box of chocolates since you never know what you're going to get. Some days I can go into the field and shoot darned near respectably. At other times, I can't hit a bear with a boat paddle.

"Shoot any birds, Bob?" It was Bill, my host. He was suddenly standing beside me. There was no time for me to collect my thoughts.

"Uhh, yeah. Well, umm, a mmmggfffm," I mumbled, nodding toward my game bag.

"What?"

"I've shot a mmmggfffm," I repeated in a low voice.

"How many did you say you have?" he asked.

"Oh, I don't know. Anyway, does it really matter, Bill?" I protested. "What matters is this beautiful day nature has provided and all this wonderful fellowship." It was too late to come clean now. I was in too deep.

"Just wondering," he replied. "They say Harvey Jr. already has seven."

"Oh."

My spirits sank even lower. Being a poor wing shot is one thing. Being a poor wing shot in the presence of a great wing shot is quite another because the difference between me (the poor shot) and that other person (the great shot) is made painfully and pitifully obvious to everyone, most of all me.

When confronted with that situation, I often tell myself that it has nothing to do with ability. Harvey Jr. is twenty-five years old, has perfect eyesight, and the lightning quick reflexes of youth. I, on the other hand, am well into middle age, afflicted with failing vision, slowing reflexes, and a half dozen other little maladies I won't even name. This rationale usually makes me feel better.

But in rare moments, when I choose to be honest with myself, I admit the truth. Harvey Jr. is what is usually referred to as a "natural." He is a born wing shot. When Harvey Jr. shoots at something, it falls as naturally as night follows day. I, on the other hand, am and always have been what might be termed an "unnatural." Whatever shooting skills I have, I've accomplished through blood, sweat, and tears. There have been no gifts. Having reached a low to medium level of proficiency, I must hang on to it with bloody fingernails. Why do I continue? Because, as General Patton said in the movie, "I love it. God help me, I do love it so."

"A lot of the fellows have four or five birds," my host continued, waking me from my self-pitying daydream.

"Oh, wonderful," I said.

"Well, I hope you limit out before this rain sets in," he said, looking up at the darkening sky. "Good luck," he called out as he started for his spot behind a small cedar tree.

Limit out indeed. I couldn't even remember the last time I'd shot fifteen doves. It had been years. Even in my youth, before I became afflicted with cross dominance and an elbow that creaks like a rusty hinge, I rarely limited out. I may as well wish for a ride on the space shuttle.

"Would you like something to drink, Mr. McDill?" a little voice asked.

It was one of my host's two small granddaughters. She and her sister were piloting a golf cart loaded with cold drinks around the field. Dressed in tiny khaki outfits, field boots, and camo slouch hats, they looked like little Hemingway dolls. Or perhaps field elves.

"A bottle of water would be nice," I said, smiling warmly.

"How many birds do *you* have, Mr. McDill?" one of them asked.

"Mmmggfffm."

"Daddy has six," she said innocently.

They whirred away toward their next stop.

A high bird went sailing over. I swung on it carefully, measuring my lead as prudently as if I had been building a bookshelf. I pulled the trigger. Two long gray tail feathers fluttered down out of the darkening sky. The bird sped on.

The first raindrops began spattering against my straw hat. The sky had blackened, and I could hear thunder approaching across the fields from the west.

Oh, well, that's the end of this outing, I thought. *Surely they'll cancel the remainder of it. It's a well-known fact that doves don't fly in the rain.*

Calling off the rest of the hunt would be a blessing. My shooting was not getting any better. When I get into one of those downhill slides, there is usually no stopping it, nothing short of a few hours on the skeet range, that is. Better to go home and sulk than to torture myself. *Anyway, what was I thinking bringing my little Fox into the dove field?* I hadn't shot the gun in years. I had set myself up, assured my own failure. And with me, it doesn't take much.

Just then a high bird came jetting over. Without thinking, I mounted the gun, swung hard, and pulled the muzzles out in front of it. When I squeezed the trigger, the bird dropped in a puff of feathers.

Darn, what do you know? There it is, I thought. That smooth, fluid swing. *Where did that come from?*

I sauntered out grandly to pick it up, as if I'd been picking up birds all afternoon. As I retrieved my prize and started back toward my position, I spotted another fast mover coming straight for me. The gun went to my shoulder instinctively, and I caught up with the bird directly overhead. It was hit dead center. If it had been a clay target, it would have been powdered. Then, to my amazement, I took a third straight bird and a fourth. The little Fox was beginning to feel like a body part. It came to my shoulder and swung through as naturally as if it had been flesh and blood. Shooting had suddenly become as effortless as pointing my finger.

Oh, you've got it now! I said to myself, feeling a surge of adrenaline and pure joy. *You've found your rhythm! You're in the zone! You're smokin,' baby!*

The rain had started falling harder. Most hunters were running out of the field toward the trees. I realized that I was getting very wet. I shot a fifth bird, a low left to right. Incredibly, the doves kept flying in spite of the downpour.

My host ran by me. For a brief moment, he stopped. "Hey, aren't you coming in?" he called out over the noise of the thunder.

"No! Yes! In a minute!" I shouted back as I took a high overhead bird.

"We're all going to the barn," he called as he dashed away, holding his hat firmly on his head with one hand.

"Okay, yeah, I'm coming."

But I didn't follow him. I couldn't. My feet were frozen, fused to the ground. I could no more have left that dove field than I could have flapped my arms and flown to New Orleans. I was shooting like a master. I didn't know why, but there it was. I was Lord Walsingham, Capt. Bogardus. And I would not give it up. Not yet. A breakneck pair went by. Effortlessly, I took the low bird first, swinging out ahead of him, knowing without a hint of a doubt when the correct lead appeared. Then I banged the high bird a split second later. It

ISTOCK

folded its wings and dropped like a stone. Still the doves kept flying. Perhaps the storm had caught them by surprise, and they were racing for the shelter of the trees.

By then, the lightning was all around me. But I was strangely unconcerned. Big, jagged bolts ripped down out of the clouds and hit the ground on every side. Thunder popped and exploded like bombs hurled out of the sky by some angry god. The rain whipped down in sheets. But I was in the zone. I could not miss. Eight, nine, ten birds were down. Eleven. I knew somehow, deep inside, that the lightning would not, could not, strike me. I was a force larger than lightning. I was invincible.

Twelve birds, thirteen birds, I was nearing that magic number, that holy grail of dove shooting. It was something I hadn't achieved in years, fifteen birds, a limit. Just as the dark clouds moved past, I took my fourteenth bird. He had slipped in behind me, and I didn't see him until it was almost too late. It was a going away shot, ordinarily a difficult one for me, but not that day.

Then the late afternoon sun broke out, and the hunters began returning to the field. As they walked by, they looked at me curiously. Then I realized that I was soaked through. My clothes were wet and heavy and clung to my skin. My panama hat was a soggy mess. And there may have been a touch of madness in my eyes.

With fourteen birds down, all I needed was one more for a limit. With only another hour or so of sunlight, I searched the sky hungrily, one more, just one more. But suddenly, incredibly, they had stopped flying. There was only an occasional single flanking the far tree line. Soon, the sun was large and orange and touching the western horizon.

"Okay, fellows, let's call it a day," Bill called out. "Let's all go to the barn and have a toast."

I didn't move.

"It will be dark soon, and I want everyone out of the field," he said after a few more minutes. "Come on, guys, let's get a move on."

Okay, I was licked. *It's over,* I thought.

Just then a single bird came flying toward me. It came on deliberately, arrow straight, through the twilight.

There it is, I said to myself. *There's my limit.*

The dove came on determinedly, on a line as straight as if it had been drawn with a ruler.

"Not yet," I whispered. "Careful, careful."

At the proper moment, I shouldered the gun and moved the barrels past the bird. As the muzzles crossed an imaginary point about twelve inches in front of my target, I pulled the trigger, exactly as I had done the last fourteen times in a row. But this time, to my astonishment, the bird kept flying. There was no reaction from the dove at all, no turn, no dodge, nothing. It simply sailed on across the darkening fields.

Oh, well, not today, I said to myself as I unloaded my shotgun and folded my stool. *You just set your sights a little too high, old boy. You got too big for your britches.*

Alone, I walked slowly out of the field, the last one to leave, and took a path through the trees. Following a light on the front of the barn, I made my way up to the oversized doorway. The inside was cavernous, the size of a gymnasium. Equipment was hung in neat rows on the walls. The farm vehicles were parked side by side and noticeably clean. It had the immaculate, well-ordered look of the gentleman farmer, the country squire. My host had set up a bar in one corner and was, himself, serving drinks to the boisterous crowd.

"Where have you been, Bob?" he called out. "I was about to send out the bloodhounds."

"Sorry, Bill."

"Get over here and have a sip of this fine Tennessee whiskey. You look like you could use it."

"I am bound by good manners to obey my host's wishes," I called back, putting on a cheerful air.

I had started across the concrete floor toward the bar when a figure dressed in camo and a baseball cap stepped out of the crowd. It was Harvey Jr. "Here, Mr. Bob, I think this belongs to you."

He tossed a bundle of feathers toward me. I caught it in my right hand and looked down at the small gray form.

"What's this?" I asked.

"That's one of your birds," he answered. "Remember the high one that you feathered just as the rain started? He fell dead on my side of the trees."

"My bird?" I asked.

"Yes, sir," he answered. "How many does that make for you anyway?"

"Fifteen," I whispered.

As I held the dove in my hand, I heard the low rumble of thunder in the distance. The storm was miles away by then, somewhere over those dark fields to the east. What had happened to me out there? For a time, I had been magnificent, flawless. For whatever crazy reason, I had shot like a legend. Then it was gone as quickly and mysteriously as it had come.

But I'm not bitter. I figure that I'm better off for the experience. Because no matter how I might struggle with my commonplace shooting ability for the rest of my years, I can always look back on that afternoon and remember what it felt like. For an hour or so, I was a natural.

17

Green Hornets

From *Shooting Sportsman*

"Teal," John whispered.

The Deacon and I came to attention, our eyes suddenly searching the horizon. We both leaned forward off the wet wooden plank that served as a bench.

"Where?" the Deacon asked.

"Out front! Get ready!"

Then I saw them. There were a dozen or so. They were 100 yards out, skimming the top of the rice straw, first in a tight bunch, then breaking apart into three separate groups of four. As I watched them, they came together again, the distance between the birds imploding as they compressed into a center, like planets being drawn into a black hole. Then again they exploded outward like a star burst, all the time soaring over the flooded field.

We were crouched inside a steel pit, four feet wide by twelve feet long, sunk four feet deep into the muddy gumbo of central Arkansas. It was at the very center of 200 acres of flooded rice stubble bordered by levees big enough to drive a truck down. Covering the pit was a steel and wire top, laced with straw and mounted on rollers. When we peeked through the narrow opening between the lip of the pit and the top, our noses were just above water level.

The birds were coming straight for us. They had seen our decoys and were intent on another look. With my right hand in a death grip, I held the handle that rolled the top back. The birds soared to the edge of our spread. But at the last minute they turned away on a dime. I came within a half second of jerking back the cover. But no.

"Not this time!" I whispered to my companions. "Not this time."

John and the Deacon were half standing, half squatting. They were poised like Olympic runners in the blocks waiting for the starting pistol. The birds sailed away over the field toward the levee. But when they reached it, they turned again and started back.

"They're coming back," I said.

On they came at top speed this time, veering far downwind and approaching our decoys from the east.

"Okay! Get ready! Get ready!"

My two companions again tensed themselves. Their rear ends lifted ever so slightly off the bench. I heard them click off the safeties on their shotguns. But I had to anticipate the flock's movements and direction. If I waited until they were actually in range to throw back the top, it would be too late. By the time I opened it and the three of us got to our feet, the birds would have passed us and been far downwind.

But they were coming straight for us.

"Get ready! Get ready!" I kept repeating insanely.

At sixty yards, I shoved back the top. We jumped to our feet. But no! At the last second, the flock turned again, barely coming within fifty yards. Still they had not seen us. It was not too late. We had to get down.

"No!" I said in a hoarse whisper, warning my companions not to shoot. "Get down!" I warned as I pulled the top back over us as fast as I could.

But John ducked a second too late.

"Holy hell, man, you almost took my head off!" he said.

"Sorry."

He rubbed the back of his head. His hunting cap lay in the mud on the pit floor.

"Good Lord, you darned near decapitated me!"

"I'm sorry, John. I'll be more careful."

The birds had still not seen us. Far out in the field, they turned again to make a last approach. This would be the one, the closest. On they came like a squadron of fighter jets executing a maneuver, pairing, splitting apart, and then coming back together. At fifty yards, I threw open the top. In an instant, they were on top of us. We jumped to our feet. I swung the muzzle of my shotgun out ahead of one of the speeding blurs and pulled the trigger instinctively. It dropped like a used up rocket. I was vaguely aware of the sound of more shots being fired behind me. But my attention was focused on my assignment. Was there a chance at another bird? By then they were going away. I swung desperately on one of the escaping forms and pulled the trigger, trying to judge the lead. It was a wasted attempt. My target soared on untouched across the flooded stubble, rejoining the rest of the flock.

"How many?" The Deacon asked excitedly.

"It looks like three out front," John answered.

"I've got one on my end," I said.

"That's four down!" the Deacon announced triumphantly.

He held up his hand for a high five. John and I both slapped his palm in return.

"Gosh, those little buggers must have been doing sixty miles an hour!" the Deacon exclaimed.

"At least," John corrected him. "When they turned downwind, it looked like they were going to break the sound barrier."

He turned Big O loose. The big Lab leapt up out of her dog box and charged through the shallow water toward the closest teal. Then seeing movement in the stubble ahead, she passed up the dead bird and galloped out to fetch the cripple. Three down out front. One of my partners had doubled. John was grinning from ear to ear. He'd forgotten all about the bump on his head.

In our area, green-winged teal fly early—early in the season and early in the morning. They don't come south as soon as their cousin the blue-wing because they can stand colder weather. But they usually arrive before the big flocks of mallards. And they're gone before the bitter cold of late season. In addition they're most active early in the morning.

For the most part, the Deacon was a mallard man. He loved to call them, watch them work, bring them into the wind, and hang them over the decoys "like Christmas tree ornaments." To him, all other ducks were merely a warm-up. John felt much the same way. But our six duck limit allowed only four mallards. To complete it, each hunter needed two other ducks or what we called "little ducks." We saw quite a few widgeons, and they are reasonably tasty. We were not particularly fond of gadwalls. But it was really no contest. Early morning became "teal time." On days when big ducks were scarce, our bird straps contained more teal than my partners would have wanted. But even a full limit of teal would have been fine with me. Secretly, that first hour or so of light became my favorite part of the day. It was a cross between a duck shoot and a circus.

They are the smallest of the puddle ducks, twelve to fourteen inches long and weighing no more than three-quarters of a pound. The drake is a spectacular little bird. His head is chestnut red and from his eyes, sweeping back

ISTOCK

to his crest, is a green mask, giving him the look of a diminutive superhero. The Green Hornet. The hen, on the other hand is a dull, speckled little duck. But she does share with the male the bright green wing patches. Some would describe them as teal green.

Other things set the little critter apart. It is not the fastest duck but is among the fastest. Yet its erratic, darting flight makes it one of the most difficult to shoot and therefore one of the most sporting. It flies like a jet-powered pigeon, darting and veering and never doing what the shooter next expects. A flight might be one bird or thirty. Seen from a distance, a big flock looks like a swarm of bees. It glides over the rice stubble, pulsing and changing shape like a cloud.

The natural inclination is to call to them, give them the old mallard highball. But they rarely respond. Even though the female makes her own crisp quacking sound, I've never seen teal pay much attention to a duck call. They are simply too busy getting from one place to another.

For me (and I'm not by myself in this), it is absolutely the best table duck of all, bar none. With all due apologies to mallard and canvasback fans, the green-winged teal beats them hands down. A plucked green-wing, with its plump round breast and layer of winter fat, looks like a store-bought Cornish game hen. The little bird isn't large enough to be sliced up and served with a sauce. It's better left whole, marinated in your favorite concoction, and quick roasted in a hot oven or over a hot grill. They should be removed a bit rare, hot pink. Served whole on a plate, they can be easily carved up with knife and fork. If nobody's watching, you can eat them like corn on the cob. They remind me of a brook trout or a hen egg, small, compact, one of nature's perfect foods.

In our duck pit, we had a new pit boss every morning. The job passed from me to John to the Deacon, back to me and so forth. It was the pit boss's duty to decide when to shoot, that is, when the ducks were in range. In the past it had been a haphazard thing. Whoever felt the urge or could no longer stand the tension simply pushed back the top, jumped to his feet, and yelled, "Let's get 'em!" But after years of arguing about ducks being called too early, too late, or too high, we finally hit on the idea of taking turns. In time we began to treat the job seriously. It became an unspoken contest between us. The number of birds bagged at the end of a day depended as much on the pit boss's judgment as on anything else.

It's teal that give the pit boss fits. One never knows, on any particular pass, whether the birds are coming close enough or not. Unlike big ducks that often get lower and closer with each approach, teal come over like guided missiles with a tailwind. Then the flock circles around the field and makes another run at you like fighter jets on a strafing mission. Open the top on the wrong pass, fire a gun, or allow the birds to see you, and you've blown it. They are not likely to come back. It's hard to keep one's cool. In the excitement, I've pushed the lid back so violently that it's been thrown completely off its tracks. Then we've had to climb out and set it back on its rollers. This while birds were overhead and my hunting partners were giving me bloody hell.

If one were to compare teal shooting to some station on a sporting clays course, it would be most like an incoming grouse or a low pheasant. The station on many courses called "springing teal" has always been a conundrum to me. At that stand, two targets are released and fly side by side, straight up for about thirty yards, until their momentum is spent. Then they fall back to the ground. I've never seen teal do anything of the sort. My irritation with that station and that particular pair of targets may be compounded by the fact that I've never been able to hit the damned things.

Another day. It is 6:00 a.m. The stars are spectacularly bright and appear to be so close one can imagine touching them with a boat paddle. In this rural setting, there is almost no light pollution. Orion, the hunter, stands low in the western sky, accompanied by his two dogs, Canus Major and Canus Minor. John, the Deacon, and I decided, on one of these clear mornings years ago, that if Orion knew what he was doing, Canus Major was a big black Lab, and Canus Minor was a Jack Russell terrier.

We have made the trek by moonlight, crossing the wide ditch by boat, then pulling the johnboat behind us, tramping the last 100 yards by foot through eighteen inches of water and another foot of black ooze. The boat is now hidden, and the three of us have climbed down into the pit. When the Deacon turns off his flashlight, there is only the half light of the moon and the sounds of gear being stowed under the bench and shotguns being loaded and snapped shut. Then silence. John is the first to speak.

"Whose turn is it?"

"What?"

"Whose turn is it to be pit boss?" he asks.

"I think it's Bob's," the Deacon answers.

"Just watch out for my head. Okay?" John says with a grin.

"I promise."

Before it is visible on the eastern edge of the earth, the sun has started to light our surroundings. We can see each other clearly now, the muddy pit floor, the empty shell casings. Then the tip of the bright yellow sphere appears above the eastern levee. The rice stubble is suddenly brilliant as if lit from within.

We stand up in the pit with the top back, wordless. It is good to be where we are, good to be alive. Big O waits in her dog box. She searches the morning sky for fowl, the only one of us who isn't captured by the sunrise. All business.

Suddenly, above our heads, there is a loud "whooosh."

"What in the heck was that?" John asks.

"Teal. They came right over us!" the Deacon answers.

"Did they see us?"

"I don't know. Let's get down."

We duck our heads and close the cover. Half standing under the low overhead, we look out through the narrow opening.

"Where are they?"

"Right out there, about two o'clock. I think they're coming back!"

I take hold of the handle that opens the top.

"Get ready!" I whisper.

18

Fast and Too Fast

From *Shooting Sportsman*

"Where is he, Mr. Charlie?"

"He's way out there on your left, John."

Charlie was standing beside me on the raised rear floorboard of the Jeep. We each had one hand on the roll bar. The backseat was a customized affair, built high over the dog kennel. He was shading his eyes with his free hand like the lookout in a crow's nest. The two of us occupied the rear while Neely, our other shooting partner, sat in front beside John Newton, our guide and dog handler.

"Well, what's he doing?"

We were watching John's rookie dog. He had been ranging far and wide all morning.

"I can't tell." Charlie answered. "He's ... no, wait a minute! Oh hell, he's locked up!"

John gunned the Jeep forward without warning. Suddenly, we were careening along the red dirt road, bouncing in and out of potholes the size of moon craters. I let go of the roll bar to grab my hat. As I did, the vehicle tossed sideways, and I came a hair's breadth from being left sitting in the road. I seized the bar with both hands and sat down like a scolded pup.

"Yeah, I see him now," the guide said as we rounded a little grove of scrub oak.

The dog stood frozen about thirty yards off the lane. John brought us to a stop.

"Okay, who's ready to rock and roll?" he asked.

We were shooting in a threesome. In that drill, one hunter sits out each covey. He functions as spotter, watching from the Jeep and marking down singles that can be hunted up after the covey rise.

"I think it's my turn to stay behind," Charlie said. "You fellas give 'em hell."

For the past fifteen seasons we had spent one weekend a year at Ashburn Hill Plantation. There in the pines of South Georgia, our group of a dozen or so long-distance friends met annually for great southern food, complementary drinks, cigars, and good shooting. We had never been disappointed. The staff and guides treated us like prodigal uncles. And always, our group took up just where we'd left off. The same inside jokes were rekindled, the same gags dusted off and started up again, and the same shooters formed themselves into pairs and threesomes.

My friend George had started it all. He had decided, years ago, that the sudden withdrawal from shooting after duck season was far too traumatic. A late winter quail hunt was the perfect way of tapering off. Ashburn Hill was our nicotine patch.

I climbed down. Neely and I arrived at the gun box at the same time. Each of us removed a slim 20 gauge side-by-side. So soon after waterfowl hunting, they looked surprisingly small. But it was Ashburn Hill policy. Old squire Frank Pidcock himself, now gone several years, had scowled at anything larger than a 20 on his plantation. And I mean that literally. Anyone showing up with a 16 or a 12 got a look from him that would curl the bark on a loblolly pine. No one ever returned the second year without a "proper" quail gun. We caught up with John, who was waiting at the edge of the grass.

"Mr. Neely, if you don't mind, walk on around that little thicket," he said. "Mr. Bob, if you'll just stay on my left, please."

One thing you had to admit about South Georgia people: they were polite. We started ahead, about twenty feet apart. Then the young pointer crept forward a step.

"Whoa, whoa," John coaxed in a low voice.

These were pen-raised quail. That mistake by the dog would've been enough to send a wild covey into the air. The truth is our noisy approach would probably have been enough. But these birds held. We stopped about four or five feet behind the dog. A wild covey never would have stood for it.

"Ready, gentlemen?" John asked.

He glanced at Neely and then at me. Each of us held our little guns at the ready, pointed skyward. Neely was a large man. In his hands, the slender 20 gauge looked like a baton in the hands of a conductor. He stood there waiting in anticipation as if he were about to bring the orchestra to attention.

Our guide started forward. On his third step the birds took to the air.

There were about a half dozen. They rose en masse, hanging together in a wad of wings and feathers. My first impulse was to shoot right into the middle of them, maybe get a lucky start on a double. Then one separated himself from the rest. He was going for the thicket. The little gun came to my shoulder, and I dropped him in a hail of feathers. Then I glimpsed another. He was motoring through the woods on my left like a Cessna. The pines were thick on that side, and it was a shot I could have passed up. I had knocked the skin off more than one tree that weekend. But it was all I had. Thankfully, I caught him in the open. I was on a roll.

"Nice double, Mr. Bob," John said.

"Thank you," I said, grinning like a Northern Shoveler.

Neely had doubled too. We picked up the two singles without any trouble. Each of us was three for three. We were as happy as a couple of teenagers with car keys.

Okay, I know they were only pen-raised quail, but these flew pretty doggone well. And I don't shoot a lot of doubles. I felt darned good about it.

It had taken me a while to get used to the idea of shooting "put out" birds.

BOB WHITE

For a long time I had turned up my nose at it. Even a mediocre shot like me wants to test himself against the real McCoy. But this trip to Ashburn Hill was always great fun. And the quail here were famous for being good fliers. Still, I was always aware that these were not the genuine article. More than once I had suggested to the group that we go down to Texas and get into some wild bobs.

There was a time when shooting released quail didn't offer much sport. In fact, it was considered downright unsporting in some quarters. Many's the old timer who came back from a day on some game farm and swore he'd never do it again.

"Half the time, they gotta kick the damn things to make them fly!" he'd say. Or, "Even if they do get up, sometimes they don't fly any farther than from here to there. They just don't act like real quail."

That was true. And in some places, under certain conditions, it still is. But if you haven't tried them lately, say in the last ten years, you might be surprised. Like so many things, it's related to economics. The boom of the last ten or fifteen years has had its effect. It seems that once a man finds he's got a few extra dollars at the end of the month, his worldview changes. He might try his first really good cigar. Then some acquaintance may tempt him with a sip of single malt Highland whiskey. Next thing you know, he's tramping through the briars in Barbour leggings with a vintage Parker under his arm. Pen-raised birds are here to stay. These days, there simply isn't enough of the real thing to go around.

But this isn't all bad. The land office business on plantations and game farms has encouraged new people to get into the quail-raising business. Competition, as every good capitalist knows, improves the product. It's all about presentation. That's the insider's word for how a well bird flies. Ideally, to give the hunter a good gunning experience, a quail should get up and go strong, fast, and hard for fifty yards or more. Exactly how much more is a matter of opinion. Lamar Sauls, who oversees such things at Ashburn Hill, prefers bobs that go the distance, 100 yards or better. "If the bird gets away, that's fine too," he says. "For us, it's not about filling up your freezer."

Quail raisers now go to great lengths in the interest of presentation. The most important innovation in the last decade has been the flight pen. This is a wire cage as much as 100 yards long. Long enough for young quail to build wing strength and stamina. Most are located outdoors so that birds can be acclimated to the elements. Contact with humans is minimal. In many cases, only one person feeds and waters these bobs, exposing them to only one human scent. This preserves their natural fear of man, or at least all those not associated with dinnertime.

Some quail growers take a different approach. Jimmy Poore of Poore Farm in South Georgia, raises his bobs in near total darkness. In theory, they are more wary when put out in the field and exposed to daylight and easier to spook. Easily spooked is a good thing when you're talking about "liberated" birds. Furthermore, they stay close to where they were released. Human contact is, again, minimal. Jimmy Poore feeds his flock each day while he wears the same white lab coat and yellow rain cap. His outfit never varies. In theory, any man or beast not wearing a white lab coat and yellow rain hat will trigger the escape response. So far he's gotten rave reviews.

From my experience, the new pen-raised birds, those raised in the last ten years, fly pretty darned well. Shooting them is nothing to be ashamed of. Of course, there are still days when you see bloopers. But it's not just how a bird was raised prior to being "put out" that determines its behavior. On any given day, temperature, rain, and even barometric pressure can have an effect.

It was our last afternoon at Ashburn Hill Plantation. We jostled along the red dirt lanes, watching the dogs, at peace with the world. I sat in front, next to John. It was a beautiful day and Neely and Charlie seemed happy and self-satisfied. Seated high in the raised rear seat, they looked like a couple of potentates, governors of the Raja in pursuit of tigers.

Just then, I caught sight of a flash of white. It was one of the dogs about seventy-five yards off the lane.

"What's he doing way down in that thicket?" I asked.

"That's a good question," John answered.

Liberated birds are usually put out pretty close to the lane. At Ashburn Hill, the guides never know exactly where they are. But a covey in thick cover seventy-five yards off the road usually means something out of the ordinary.

The dog was half obscured by bracken, but he was clearly on point, his tail high. John stopped the Jeep and sat watching him for a moment. Then he turned to us and whispered, "wild covey."

I felt a thrill go through me, a little extra surge of adrenaline. This was the real thing, not some put out, pen-raised imitation. It was not unusual to find wild birds at Ashburn Hill. But I hadn't hit on a native covey in a couple of seasons. It was a chance to really test my skills, to put the old chops on the line.

An old memory came flooding back to me. I was twelve years old, and the proud owner of my first shotgun. It was a little youth model, a bolt action 410 with bright red and green buttons by the safety indicating safe and fire. My two friends and I had followed their two beagles into the center of a winter rice field. There was a push down there, a tangle of bulldozed trees and scrub, thick with trumpet vine and blackberry. That's where the rabbit had led us. The dogs nosed into the cover, howling and yelping. My friends spread out to the sides, hoping to be ready when the bunny made its exit. That left me in the middle, facing the sun.

Suddenly there was a roar of wings. Two or three dozen quail erupted from the tangle like a swarm of hornets. Without any conscious effort on my part, the little shotgun came to my shoulder. I took the first bird easily. As it sailed to the right, I needed only to overtake it to bring it down. I worked the bolt. Then I saw another, flying straight into the yellow light. I squinted my eyes and pointed at the place the bird had disappeared. When I pulled the trigger, it dropped out of the sun like some tiny fallen god. I had doubled on wild birds.

"You coming?" Charlie asked.

"Yeah, sure," I answered.

It was Neely's turn to spot. Charlie and I eased down off the Jeep. I took my little 20 out of the gun box and closed the lid without making a sound. We joined John out front. At his signal, we started our approach. Instead of marching forward, we almost tiptoed. This was John's best dog. He didn't move a muscle. But of course, these bobs had been hunted. They would be skittish. At about twenty yards, farther out than I had anticipated, it happened.

"Kawhooosh!" Up they came. But this time, to my amazement, they seemed to shoot out of the briars as if fired from a gun. To my eyes, they didn't even look like quail. They were blurs. Neither did they rise into the air. Instead, each bird seemed slung outward as if by centrifugal force. The covey was like a wheel spinning apart. I tried to point my muzzles at one feathered form and found that it had vanished. There were two reports from Charlie's side, but in the confusion, I couldn't find a shot. I was like a football player who's been going through drills all summer at half speed, and suddenly finds himself in a real game. Then I saw a single flying straight away. It was already at about thirty yards and making its way through the naked pine trees like a scud missile. I covered it up and pulled the trigger. It didn't fall. Desperately, I let go the second barrel. By then it was at the limit of my range. It disappeared into the woods. I looked back to where the birds had risen a half second before. They were gone, all of them.

"You've got one down, don't you, Mr. Charlie?" I heard John ask.

"I believe I do," Charlie answered.

"Did you get one, Mr. Bob?"

"No. No, I didn't," I said.

Maybe I'm not fast enough to shoot native quail anymore. Perhaps it's something that happens to a man in middle age, something irreversible. No, I refuse to accept that. I've simply *allowed* myself to slow down. We do that, you know, unconsciously, the way a bunny matches his speed to the hounds. Without realizing it, I've let my reflexes slow to the pace of pen-raised birds. That's not to say I can't get my edge back. A couple of days on the skeet range and then some real wild bird hunting ought to do it. I'll go down to Texas, get into old Mr. Bob White himself. Get the old hand-eye back up to the mark, get sharp.

I can see it now, standing behind the dogs under that big blue western sky as those game little rockets explode out of the grass, ripping through the clear air at the speed of light, like images on double exposed film, jetting past me before I've hardly had time to get my gun to my shoulder ... On the other hand, there's no shame these days in shooting pen-raised birds.

19

Four Feet Down

A descent into the dark underworld of duck hunting

From *Shooting Sportsman*

"Shhhhh!"

"What?"

"I heard a quack," the Deacon whispered.

"Are you sure?" I asked.

"Of course I'm sure," he said. "I know what a quack sounds like."

I twisted my neck and squinted through the narrow slit. The sky above us was bright and winter blue.

"Where are they?" John asked

"I don't know where they are," the Deacon answered.

"You didn't see them?"

"No, I didn't see them. How could I possibly see anything through this blasted top?"

"Why don't we pull it back and have a look?" I asked.

"No! If you open the top they'll see *us*," John scolded.

"I can't be expected to call ducks properly when I don't know where they are or what they're doing," the Deacon announced indignantly.

"Yeah? Well, if you can't see them, they can't see you," John countered.

"You guys put too much straw on top this year," the Deacon went on. "It's like a freakin' tomb in here. I feel like Edgar Allan damned Poe."

"There they are, out front!" John interrupted, peeping through the narrow opening.

The ducks were 100 yards out and working into the wind. A half-dozen mallards were milling low over the rice stubble. Big O looked out at them from her dog box. She stared through the same small crack, trembling in anticipation. The Deacon started with a "welcome" call, not too much, considering the birds' distance. Next came a series of soft quacks. As they got closer, he segued into a feed chuckle. Suddenly, they caught the wind and gained altitude.

"I've lost them. Where are they?"

"I think they're on your end," I said, straining my neck to look out.

"I don't see them anywhere." John said, trying his best to see through the thick layer of rice straw.

"Well, *somebody* tell me where they are!" the Deacon whispered desperately.

John eased the top back a couple of inches and peeped out.

After a minute, he opened it enough to put his head through. "They're gone," he said.

"Holy Nash Buckingham!" the Deacon bellowed. "I had those ducks on a string! I had them hooked! How is a man expected to call ducks when he can't even see them? If I had known they were turning away, I would have blown a comeback." He kicked the wall of the pit with his rubber boot. "This is the most damnable and godforsaken contrivance ever associated with the sport of waterfowling!"

He was right. A pit is the most frustrating, neck-twisting, claustrophobia-inducing abomination from which to hunt ever invented. But in the vast, flat rice fields of central Arkansas, where anything that sticks up higher than a breadbox will flare birds, it's the only way. Ours measured four feet wide by twelve feet long by four feet deep. Most of its four feet of depth was buried in the Arkansas mud. When the water surrounding it was at its proper depth, it came to only a few inches below the lip. The cover was mounted on rollers and made of steel and welded wire. For purposes of concealment, this was blanketed with a thick layer of rice straw. The whole business stuck up less than a foot. But to camouflage it even further, the pit was incorporated into a long row of stubble.

It would accommodate four hunters comfortably. When I say comfortably, I only mean that when four men sat side by side on the wooden plank, there was adequate elbow room. In a pinch you could squeeze in five. But the low cover provided for very little headroom. Visibility was limited to the narrow space under the sliding cover. When looking through that opening, one's nose was just above water level. It was a bunker, a hole in the ground. Sometimes it felt like a coffin.

"How about a seventh inning stretch?" I said.

"I thought you'd never ask," the Deacon said.

We rolled back the cover and stood up. The sky was clear, and a frigid, fresh wind was blowing. It felt glorious to be above ground in the light and fresh air, to stretch our limbs.

"Gee, my neck is killing me," the Deacon complained, rubbing under the collar of his hunting coat.

"Mine too," John said.

We called it "pit neck." By the end of a hunt, we all had it. Imagine sitting on a bench for four or five hours with only an inch or two of headroom, unable to stand or stretch. Add to this the head turning, neck twisting, and peep holing required to track the movement of overhead ducks. One needed a masseur.

"Ducks!" I interrupted. "Get down!"

High and approaching from the southeast were about two dozen mallards. We ducked and rolled the top forward. The birds hadn't seen us.

I checked our spread. How did it look? Peering out through the crack, I saw the decoys were just at eye level, bobbing on the choppy surface. We had waded through them not a half hour before, and the water still appeared muddy and disturbed. Good. The Deacon was blowing his hail call now, a five-note descending song. John was backing him up, filling in the background between the Deacon's entreaties.

"Where are they?" The Deacon asked breathlessly between calls.

"I was hoping you knew," John said, twisting his head in every direction.

"There!" I whispered, pointing my finger straight up.

I was on my knees on the floor of the pit, attempting to get a better angle of visibility. Through a tiny opening, I could just see them overhead. They turned and sailed downwind and out of my vision. A moment later, they reappeared far out in front of us, seemingly headed for parts unknown. But as the ducks were about to cross the levee, the lead susie cut left, turning.

"Yes!" I whispered.

"We got 'em!" the Deacon hissed, his eyes growing wide.

The others followed. The flock turned back east, starting a wide arc. As the Deacon switched to a series of pleading tones, John chuckled and quacked. I reached for my duck call and then changed my mind, putting it back in my shirt pocket. I would only get in the way. The birds circled again and again, each time closer to the edge of our spread. Now I could see the colors, the iridescent heads and specula, the white tail flashes.

"Come on, come on, come on," I heard myself whispering like a lunatic.

Then they cut sharply, turning into the wind. It was my turn to call the shot. I felt the adrenaline

"Get 'em!" I shouted, throwing back the top.

They were strung out over our decoys like targets in a shooting gallery, each bird pumping the air to gain altitude. I took the only shot I had at a big green head quartered off my corner. He appeared to be suspended, hanging in the blue sky as fixed as the flag on top of a courthouse. I aimed directly at him and pulled the trigger. My pattern only clipped a few tail feathers. In my excitement, I had, once again, fallen for this optical illusion. The duck was not fixed at all, but climbing skyward. On the second shot (the bird was higher now), I swung the muzzle past him, and when the barrel blotted him out, I pulled the trigger. This time, he fell like a rock.

The remaining birds had turned their tails and switched on the afterburners. John and the Deacon were hammering away. I tried to swing on the last one in the flock. But before I caught up with it, I realized my barrels were crowding the Deacon on my right. My muzzle was much too close to his ear. I didn't shoot. In a pit, you can lose what little hearing you have left, to say nothing of the goodwill of your friends.

"How many did we get?" the Deacon shouted.

"I see three in the decoys and one way out."

"Great calling, Deacon!" John gushed.

"You sounded awful good yourself!" the Deacon returned happily.

"And you timed the shot perfectly, Bob," they both said, grinning.

"Thanks."

When things went well, we were quite complimentary of each other. John unfastened the tether from Big O's collar and gave a command. She leapt up out of the dog box and charged past the three dead birds in pursuit of the escaping cripple. There were about eighteen inches of water and another six inches of soft mud in the field. But the big Lab was a veteran of this terrain. She loped across the flooded expanse like a whitetail deer, appearing to give herself no time to sink into the pliant muck. It was in marked contrast to the slow, labored movement required of humans to traverse this ground. Finally, at about 100 yards, she caught up with the escaping bird. After a quick confrontation, she snatched it up and started loping back.

"Thank the Lord for puppy dogs," the Deacon said seriously.

Soon all four birds were in the pit. Then came the ordeal of getting Big O back in her dog box. It was never easy. She could out-wrestle most grown men. After much pulling and coaxing, she finally agreed to step back down into the little cubicle on the right end. Then John pulled the top over us, committing us, once again, to half darkness. Big O squirmed and complained. She hated it. Who could blame her?

I put another shell in my battered autoloader and leaned it against the wall. The old contraption looked like something from the Napoleonic Wars. But this was no place for a fine shotgun. Only someone with more money than good sense would bring an expensive gun into an Arkansas duck pit. First of all there are, invariably, several inches of soupy water and mud on the floor. And there's no place to rest a gun without placing the stock in that same muck. The rice straw above your head is for concealment only, offering no protection from the weather. Then there is the 200-yard march required to get to the pit in the first place. Putting your front foot down in the soft mud is always less difficult than pulling your back foot out. I have lost my balance and fallen more than once, taking my shotgun with me.

There are, of course, inexpensive double guns. I always brought one along on my Arkansas trips as a surefire backup. But the truth is, it is difficult to use a double gun in this confined space. Even if you manage to break it open, load it, and snap it shut inside the cramped enclosure, you are left pointing a loaded gun at a steel wall a few inches from your neighbor's chest. Holding the gun outside the pit is difficult since the lip comes almost to your shoulders. Climbing outside each time you wish to reload is out of the question. On the other hand, a pump or automatic can be loaded with the muzzle pointed straight up.

In that rugged environment, inexpensive American waterfowlers find their proper role. Each of us had with him his own scarred and battered version, pumps and autos, with nicknames like Dr. Death, Sandman, and Mr. Meat. These shotguns had been used for everything from boat paddles to ice breakers, and sometimes even to break up dogfights. Breaking up dogfights usually meant stopping Big O before she dismembered some unsuspecting male dog.

My waterfowler was a Browning A-5 built in 1955. When I found it in 1980, it had hardly been fired a dozen times and looked essentially brand new. Now, twenty abusive seasons later, the barrel and receiver have the dull patina of a buffalo nickel. The stock is a road map of dents, scars, scratches, and scrapes. Halfway into my second year with the gun, it had started giving me problems. About every third time I fired it, it failed to eject the empty. A local gunsmith was kind enough to work me in, midseason. When I picked it up, he looked at me quizzically.

"What have you been doing with this thing?"

"What do you mean?" I asked.

"I got enough mud out of it to plant a garden."

"Oh."

Since then, I've had it taken apart, cleaned, and reassembled after each duck season. No more problems.

Spending that much time together in such a small space can be trying. I would advise anyone planning to share a pit with someone to make sure their friendship is rock solid. Ticks and eccentricities can loom large after a while. What once was a tiny wart can rankle into a festering carbuncle. It's like waiting out World War III in a bomb shelter with your next-door neighbor.

But good things come to the surface too. I remember one morning in particular when we'd had an unusually good start. Big O had done her job beautifully, making several long retrieves, like the dependable yeoman she was. Or would that be yeowoman? I was the only one who'd remembered a duck strap that morning so the job of keeping track of birds and limits had naturally fallen to me. Half an hour after sunrise there were already four green heads and three fat teal on my strap. The birds were hanging from a peg directly in front of me. But after putting them on the strap, I had paid little attention. Ducks were overhead constantly.

"Will you please kill that bird?" John suddenly shouted.

"What?"

"Kill that bird! Can't you see it's still alive?"

One of the teal on the strap flapped its wings just then, struggling.

"Yes, sure, John. I hadn't noticed."

"I don't see how you guys can allow something to suffer that way!" he scolded, his face red with anger.

"Sorry," I said.

Ironically, John was a dentist. He had single-handedly disproved the myth that dentists enjoy inflicting pain. On the contrary, he couldn't bear to see any creature, human or otherwise, suffer. When one of his dogs was injured or overtired, he cared for it with the tenderness of a doting mother. Understandably, he was the best dentist in town. I had long ago given him the nickname Painless, which had stuck, at least among his hunting friends.

The sun has been up an hour. It's a mallard day, cold, bright, glittering. Overhead, birds can detect the slightest movement below. We have piled fresh rice straw on top and pulled the cover tightly shut. We wait patiently, peering

ALAN PHILLIPS

now and then through tiny holes in the straw and through the narrow slit under the cover.

In the half darkness, the Deacon finally speaks, "Hey, I've been thinking about something."

"What?"

"What if we couldn't get this top open?"

"Oh, don't be silly."

"No, seriously. What if we couldn't get it open one day? We could stay out here forever. No one would ever think to come looking for us."

"There's no way we could ever get trapped in here," John answered.

"Yes, but suppose we did. It would be like being buried alive."

"You're giving me the willies," I said.

"Shhhhh!" the Deacon interrupted.

"What?"

"I heard a quack! There are ducks overhead!"

"Where are they?"

"How should I know? I can't see a blasted thing."

20

An Abundance of Snows

From *Shooting Sportsman*

"Keep your head down," Chris whispered.

I obeyed, ducking my head below the top of the levee in front of me. In a crouch, Chris moved crablike up the line to the man on my left.

"Keep your head down," I heard him say.

There were ten of us counting our three guides, spaced about twenty feet apart, crouched in a drainage ditch in the predawn darkness. The trench stretched as straight as a chalk line from the road to the woods, cutting the field in half. We were like World War I doughboys, waiting in knee-deep mud for some dawn cataclysm.

"Don't shoot till we get the word," Chris whispered.

He looked down the line to where Dusty Binford was crouched. Dusty was head guide and ramrod of our little outfit. When the time came to shoot, he would tell us. His assistants, Chris and T. Bone, were a couple of young bucks who spent most of the year employed as cowboys. Dusty had at least thirty years on the two youngsters. They addressed him as Mr. Binford.

A faint hint of gold appeared on the edge of the horizon. In a moment, I could make out things that an instant before were hidden in darkness. I saw the Texas prairie stretching away in every direction as flat as a tabletop. And about 200 yards in front of us in the dry stubble sat a sea of snow geese. It was the first weekend in December, and the big flocks had arrived in the Eagle Lake area of South Texas. I watched as a bird lifted into the air and then settled back down to earth as if it had changed its mind. Finally, when the sun had climbed an inch or so off the horizon, a few dozen geese took flight. When they had ascended ten or twelve feet, they seemed to hesitate, suspended in the stiff breeze, not sure of their purpose. Then a dozen more rose to join them. A moment later, 100 more lifted off, honking and calling loudly. In an instant, the earth itself seemed to rise up in front of us. The entire flock went up with a roar. As the flight reached an altitude of seventy-five yards or so, it began to turn on itself like a forming hurricane. Then what looked like the beginning of the mass started toward the ditch. I crouched a little lower and put my thumb on the safety of my old Browning. The first birds were now overhead. They were high but not completely out of range. I looked back at Dusty. There was no word. Now, we were beneath the midst of the flock. The sky was blanketed with geese.

"Get 'em!" Dusty shouted suddenly.

Our line exploded in gunfire. For me, the temptation was to point up into the rabble and jerk the trigger. I resisted the urge and picked out a single bird moving straight in. When I fired, it dropped like a loaf of bread. Then I spotted another one, higher. I swung out ahead of him. But not enough. The geese had gained more altitude now and were veering away from our guns. I found what looked like one last target, a high bird over my left shoulder. My shot probably trailed him by several feet. I lowered the gun and watched the flock retreat over the treetops. Chris was standing beside me.

"How many did you get, Mr. Bob?"

"Just one."

"We didn't exactly slaughter 'em," he said.

It was true. We'd shot six geese; six out of heaven knows how many thousands. There is a better way to hunt snows. In the morning, we would put it into practice.

After lunch at a roadside barbecue joint, we went back to our lodging, a small drafty farmhouse. The little house appeared to be the only structure on the prairie within a five-mile radius. Most of my friends were intent on a nap. They settled into their bunks, snoring like a bunch of wet dogs in front of a fireplace. Dusty and T. Bone had disappeared. I sat on the lumpy sofa cleaning mud out of my gun.

"You wanna ride with me, Mr. Bob?" Chris asked.

"Where are we going?"

"Looking for geese."

The gun could wait. I enjoyed Chris's company. He was a likable, well-mannered young man, the kind Middle America seems to do an outstanding job of raising. We climbed into his pickup and headed off down a two-lane blacktop. The earth stretched away as level as a game board. A voice came over the walkie-talkie on the dashboard. It was Dusty.

"Where you at, Chris?" he asked.

"About a mile south of the house," Chris answered.

"Listen, when them fellows wake up, I'm gonna take 'em down to the sporting clays course and try to keep 'em happy. You and T. Bone find some geese."

"Yes, sir."

Chris hung up and looked over at me. "If we don't find another flock, your buddies are gonna be pissed."

"Oh, they'll get over it. What about that bunch this morning? Where'd they go?"

"Who knows? Out of the county maybe." He cut a small square off the edge of a cake of tobacco and placed it behind his lower lip. "Too bad we had to pass shoot that flock," he said apologetically. "There was no time to put out rags."

"How big do you think it was?" I asked. "About how many geese?"

"Oh, maybe twenty thousand."

It was hard to imagine. But it was true. And from all indications, the flocks are getting even bigger. The snow goose population has roughly tripled over the last twenty years. And it continues to increase by about five percent a year. Four and a half million breeding birds now descend on their nesting grounds in Canada each summer. Those fragile Arctic and sub-Arctic coastal marshes can't support that many geese. Certain areas along the coast of West Hudson Bay now look like a moonscape and may take years to recover. Others are severely damaged. Breeding populations are now starting to move inland, threatening freshwater marshes.

Some biologists claim the exploding numbers may be tied to a single event. Several decades ago, the snow goose began supplementing its traditional wild diet with cultivated grain. When it did, it found an unlimited food supply in North America's great grain belt, which stretches from central Canada to Mexico. Like my old Daddy used to say, "If you want something to grow, feed it." He was talking about state government, but I suppose the principle still applies. Population numbers have responded exponentially. The snow goose hasn't wholly given up its natural diet, however, only augmented it. A big flock can still turn a grassy pasture into a mud hole.

Wildlife authorities have instituted desperate measures to reduce bird numbers. Some states and provinces now hold a spring hunting season. Electronic calls, Sunday hunting, and increased limits are allowed in many areas.

Geese start arriving in the Eagle Lake area of South Texas in mid-October. By Thanksgiving, the area is inundated. The goose season is split into two parts. During the first half, from the first week of November until the third week of January, *all* geese may be taken. During the second half, which lasts until the end of March, only snows, blues, and Ross's geese are permitted. This is called the conservation season, during which electronic calls are allowed. Even though the season ends in late March, outfitters rarely hunt past the first week of February. "They're just too damned smart by then," Dusty said. The daily limit on snows is now twenty birds, and there is no possession limit.

Among geese, the snow is, unfortunately, not the top table bird. That title, in my opinion, belongs to the Specklebelly or white fronted goose. A plucked snow always has a rather scrawny look with its prominent breastbone. Perhaps overpopulation is a factor. But carcasses are invariably less meaty and absent of fat. Even so, a young snow, properly prepared, can be tasty. Still, some people show them no respect at all. When someone downed a snow out of our old Arkansas duck pit, my partner, the Deacon, would invariably say, "There's one for the gumbo."

After a fruitless afternoon of searching, Chris dropped me at the farmhouse. As I was climbing down out of the truck, a voice came over the walkie-talkie.

"Hey, Chris! Chris, you there? I got geese, man!"

Chris grabbed the microphone. "Yeah, T. Bone. How many?"

"A freaking butt load, man! This is a big one!"

"I'll see you in the morning, Mr. Bob," Chris said. "Me and T. Bone got work to do."

That evening, Dusty drove us into El Campo for dinner. I could see that he had made quite an impression on my friends that afternoon. They now seemed to regard him as some kind of mythic hero. Dusty wasn't only a goose guide, he also worked out west and in the far north. His age was hard to guess. But with his tall crowned Western hat, neatly tied neckerchief, and wire spectacles, he looked 100 years out of time, as if he belonged in some grainy photograph taken on the Goodnight Trail about 1890.

When we walked in the front door of the restaurant, I was surprised to see that it was crowded. In all the miles and roads Chris and I had driven that afternoon, I'd seen only a handful of houses. But the place was packed. It appeared to be a combination saloon, dance hall, and cafe. But later I found the menu was made up mostly of Continental dishes. And there was a wine list as long as your leg. Nothing in Texas should ever surprise me. After inspecting a few buffalo heads and a mounted rattlesnake, I sat down at our table. Dusty was into another story. My hunting companions were listening with eager attention.

"So, I'm guiding this Prince Rupert and his people up in Alaska for bear," he said. "Well, about two days out, a couple of them fellows come to me and, they say, 'Hey, you got to start showing Prince Rupert the proper respect.' I says, 'what do you mean'? And they say, 'You can't call him Rupert anymore. From now on you got to address him as Your Highness.'"

Dusty paused a moment to allow this to sink in. The circle of admirers around the table waited for the punch line, which they seemed sure was coming.

"So ..." Dusty began, drawing out the moment. "I said, boys, I guided Roy Rogers. And if I can call him Roy, I ain't calling nobody Your Highness."

The table exploded in laughter, all except Dusty who kept an appropriately straight face. The story wasn't only funny. There was something satisfying about it. Dusty had perfectly expressed our American view of titled nobility.

The next morning I lay on the cold ground covered with a white bed sheet. My old Browning humpback lay beside me under the sheet like a familiar old spouse in a marriage bed. But it was a cold bed indeed. With no ground cloth beneath me, the chill was already making its way numbingly into my bones. The sheet was merely camouflage. From the air I suppose I looked like a patch of unmelted snow or perhaps a very large goose. Around me, hundreds of white garbage bags fluttered noisily in the freshening breeze.

If snow geese were easy to bag, there wouldn't be 4.5 million of them. They are wary and hard to fool. It's difficult to bring these birds into a field they're not familiar with. The best way to hunt them is to find out where they want to go and get there a little ahead of them.

It had been light an hour when I saw them. They appeared at first like a stratum of smog on the sunlit horizon. Then the layer began to grow larger, rising above the earth's edge until it looked like an approaching storm cloud. Soon I could hear them, or rather it, since there were no singular honks, cackles, or calls, only a steadfast roar like white noise. They were coming straight for us, straight for our field and the huge half circle of white fluttering flags.

BOB WHITE

When the first of the birds reached our spread, they began turning above us like a gathering weather cell. With each spiral, the swarm descended a little lower. But this was the only vanguard. The balance of the bunch was still moving in from the south like a host of biblical locusts. Later, Dusty would estimate this flock at fifty thousand.

If I had been our senior guide, I might have lost my nerve. Under the circumstances, I could have called the shot too early. Considering the inexperience of most of the shooters, any one of us could have moved or exposed himself, flaring the geese and sending them back downwind without a shot being fired. Who knew how long these hunters could lie still? I lay on my back, motionless, peeping out through a tiny opening in the sheet. The birds seemed to be moving at a maddeningly slow speed. Our three guides were honking and clucking away. Dusty alone sounded like a half dozen geese.

Finally, the sky above me was an ocean of fowl stretching from horizon to horizon. Now I could see their heads turning, their necks craning, their eyes searching the ground for anything out of order. Then a single bird touched down in the center of our spread.

I heard Dusty yell, "let's get 'em!"

I threw back the sheet, pointed the shotgun at a bird directly overhead, and pulled the trigger. It dropped like a stone. Then I was on my feet. For several seconds there was eerie silence as the geese clawed the air for altitude. I picked out another, higher but within range. The muzzle of the shotgun covered it a second before I yanked the trigger. It came down like a piece of windfall fruit. My companions were blazing away. It was raining geese. One fell just behind me and hit the earth with a thud. The roar started up again. I picked out a third target, high overhead. But I trailed it, and it slipped away with only the loss of a few tail feathers. Now the birds were gaining sky. I reached into my coat, grabbed a handful of shells, and started trying to push them into the old Browning. My hand was unsteady. Several shells fell at my feet. A huge hole had opened in the middle of the flock directly overhead. Still, I found a lone bird moving right to left, lower than the rest. I pushed the barrel past it and jerked the trigger. It tumbled. I looked for another shot. But there were none. It was over. The mass moved away south surprisingly quickly, the roar diminishing in the distance.

Small groups of geese continued to work our spread all morning, but nothing to equal that first flock. At noon, Dusty ordered us to unload. Afternoon hunting is prohibited not by law, but by mutual agreement between guides and landowners who want to keep the big flocks in the area. Most of us ended the morning's shoot with more birds than we could carry.

Two months later, I got a phone call from Chris.

"Mr. Bob, it's Chris. Mr. Binford asked me to call you."

"Oh, hello, Chris. How are you? And how's Dusty?"

"Fine. He's in Canada right now guiding some bigshot from South America. Listen, we thought you might want to come hunt with us again next fall."

It hadn't occurred to me to go back to Texas. But it had been a hell of an experience. Maybe once more. I stalled for time while searching for my date book.

"Listen, Chris, are they going to allow Sunday hunting?"

"I don't know."

"What's the limits going to be?"

"No word on that yet."

"Anybody else I know coming?"

"You're the first one I've called."

"I see."

There was silence between us as I looked for a likely weekend.

"Mr. Bob, there's only one thing I'm sure of," Chris said.

"What's that?"

"There's gonna be a hell of a lot of snow geese."

21

Low Budget Pheasants

From *Shooting Sportsman*

It all began when I made the phone call. You might call it a sympathy call or maybe a show of support. It's the kind of thing one friend does for another. Word was going around that Hawkeye Vaughan had run into some trouble.

"It's been tough," he moaned. "First, the real estate market went punk. Then my secretary ran off with my partner. Now, on top of everything else, there's this audit."

"I'm sorry, old man," I consoled. "I called to tell you your friends are behind you."

"Thanks. It's just not easy keeping the old spirits up," he said, his voice trailing off.

"If there's anything I can do," I pledged, "Don't hesitate to ask."

"I'm glad you said that," he declared, suddenly brightening. "As a matter of fact, what I really need is a little trip. You know, a few days out west under the big sky. A South Dakota pheasant hunt would be just the thing. I think if I could get out there for a while, I could be renewed, reborn."

"Okay," I said. "Count me in. When are we going?"

"Well, that's just it, old partner. I'm up to my ears here. I don't have time to scratch. Do you think maybe you could handle the logistics? You'd be saving my life."

"All right. I guess I could put the trip together. How much do we want to spend, I mean each man?"

"Well, as you know, things are a little tight here at Hawkeye Incorporated. I can't go over ..." he named a ridiculously low figure.

"You mean plane fare and everything?"

"Yeah, that's all I can manage right now. But you know, it doesn't have to be anything fancy. Just lots of good birds."

I had opened my big mouth. "If there's anything I can do," I'd said. *Okay, maybe if I add three more people,* I thought, *make it a trip for five hunters.* The cost per man would be pretty small. I called up Buddy (no relation) Vaughan, George (Pirogue) Payne, and Dr. John (Painless) Farringer. George and Buddy were in.

"Okay, I'll go," John said. "Just one thing. Make sure we get to see some good dog work."

"Sure," I said confidently. No problem."

I began poring over outdoor magazines and internet sites. There was no such thing as three days of pheasant shooting for what Hawk-eye wanted to spend. Then just when I was about to give up, I spotted a tiny box on the last page of a magazine.

LARRY'S

I've Got Birds

Come On Out

Below that were a ridiculously low per-day price and a South Dakota phone number. With renewed hope, I called.

A grizzled voice answered, "Larry's."

"Is this Larry?"

"Yep. I've got birds. Come on out."

"Listen, Larry. Do you mind if I ask you a couple of questions?"

"Are you with the government?"

"No."

"Then go ahead."

"I've got a party of five. What about accommodations?"

"Yep, we can put you up, and Ma can feed you. But it'll cost you an extra $10 a day."

I had to admit it was within our budget.

"One other thing. What about dogs?"

"Sure, I got a dog."

"Really?" I said, feeling better. "What kind of dog is it?"

"Well, sir, he's one of them Weimerweesers."

"I've never heard of that kind."

"Never mind. You and them fellers just get yourselves out here. I've got birds. I'll show you pheasants as thick as fleas on a Weimerwee ... uh, a hound dog."

I had no choice. I booked the trip and arranged for our plane tickets and rental car. The night before we were to leave, I came home and found a message on my machine.

"Hey, pal, this is Hawkeye. Sorry, I can't make the hunt tomorrow. Something big's come up. You fellows go on without me."

I could've killed him.

By the time we landed in Mitchell, South Dakota, my spirits had improved.

"Look on the bright side, fellows," I said to my companions. "So, Hawkeye let us down. At least we don't have to worry about pinching pennies anymore." As we approached the rent-a-car desk, I had an idea. "Say, how about upgrading us to a nice roomy van," I said to the agent.

"Sorry, we're all out of the vans."

"Do you have a full-sized car?"

"All out."

"A midi?"

"Sorry."

Putting four large men with guns and gear inside a Ford Escort is like putting four pounds of beans in a one-pound bag. If Hawkeye had come along, we would have had to tie him on top.

"Hey, John, how about passing me one of those oatmeal cookies?" I asked.

"Sorry, I can't."

"Why not?"

"I can't move my arms."

"That's nothing," Buddy said, not wanting to be outdone. "I can't feel anything from the waist down."

A hundred miles west, we found our marker, a hand-lettered sign directing us down a dirt lane. We pulled up beside a tidy white farmhouse set among a grove of cottonwoods.

"Hey, this doesn't look so bad," George said hopefully.

"Matter of fact, it looks damned cozy," Buddy agreed.

The screen door slammed, and a tall, lanky scarecrow of a man came striding out. He wore stovepipe jeans, a faded plaid shirt, and a ball cap that said, "Farmers Know The Best Dirt."

"Hey, I'm Larry," he said, poking his head in the front window and displaying a set of bare pink gums. "Kind of crowded in there, ain't it?"

"Yes, it is. Mind if we get out?"

"You ain't staying here."

"But you said you and Ma ..."

"You're staying at the lodge."

"Ah, of course. The lodge," my partners and I repeated, smiling at each other approvingly.

"It's at the end of this road," Larry said, pointing ahead. "Ma and me eat supper at six," he called out as we pulled away.

The lodge turned out to be a rusted house trailer dating from the 1930s. It was perched on a knoll in the middle of a sea of prairie grass. On top was a tall TV mast, giving the trailer, as it leaned to one side, the look of a leaky schooner sinking into the earth. The inside was outfitted with a half dozen army bunks and a rusty electric wall heater. Dinner that evening was a sandwich prepared by Ma. No one was sure what kind of sandwich it was. John suggested Spam. As a longtime trout fisherman, I'm intimately familiar with Spam. It wasn't Spam. After dinner, we were invited to look through Ma's scrapbooks. These were collections of Polaroids she had taken of other hunters and hunting parties. They all seemed to be looking into the camera with the same bewildered possum in the headlights look.

The next morning, Larry showed up in a battered station wagon. He was wearing the same clothes he'd had on the night before except for a pair of very large tennis shoes and a bright orange baseball cap. This one read: "Farming—I Dig It." A large gray dog was asleep on the front seat.

"Pile in, fellers!" he said.

We bounced across a half mile of prairie and through a farm gate. Then we began driving up the edge of one cornfield and down another. After about fifteen minutes, John's curiosity overcame him.

"Oh, Larry?"

"Yep?"

"Uh, I was just wondering. What are we doing?"

"Doing? Hell, son, we're pheasant huntin'!"

Just then, he stomped the brakes, sending my head banging into the seat in front of me.

"There's one! Let's get him!" he yelled.

In a second, he was out the car door and loping toward the cornfield. About twenty yards out, he stopped and looked back.

"Hey, ain't you fellers comin'?"

After a few seconds of indecision, we climbed out and began filling our pockets with shells. We joined Larry at the edge of the field. Then John noticed that the dog was still curled up on the front seat of the station wagon.

"Say, aren't you going to bring the dog?"

"Naw, he don't hunt."

"He doesn't hunt? Why not?"

"Don't know. Just never cared for it."

"Oh," John said. Then, trying to put a cheerful spin on things, he said, "So it's to be a drive, huh? What about blockers?"

"What?" Larry asked.

"Blockers. You know, men to stand at the end of the field and keep the birds from running out."

"Did you bring any with you?"

"No."

"Then we ain't got any. Spread out, fellers!"

We did as he instructed. He took the middle position. The rest of us flanked him, each of us about four corn rows apart. Larry started us out, setting the pace. He moved like some mad power walker, crashing forward through knee-high grass and ten-foot-tall cornstalks. His whiskered chin was pointed forward like the cowcatcher on a steam engine.

"There he goes! Faster!" he shouted.

I was breathing hard, pushing through tall grass, stumbling over dirt clods, and being slapped in the face by cornstalks. It was all I could do to keep up. Then I heard a cackle, a roar of wings. To my left, a cock pheasant took to the air. I glimpsed the blue-green iridescent feathers on its head as it vaulted skyward.

"There he is! Blast him!" Larry yelled.

The bird must have been right in front of him. In the thick cover, no one else had a clear view. Two shots sounded to my left, but the bird sped on.

When he cleared the stalks, I sent a Hail Mary after him without mussing a feather. Larry started forward again. When he'd gone another few yards, we came to a wire fence. He vaulted over it like an Olympic hurdler. The rest of us followed as best we could. We crossed a grassy strip and then crashed into the next field, flanking him again and pushing hard to keep up.

"Gawldernit!" I heard him say through the cover on my left.

"Dagnabit!" he murmured a moment later.

I realized then that I was carrying a shotgun and shell bag. I was wearing winter clothes, a heavy coat, and boots. My breath was coming faster now, and my pulse was racing. I began to wonder how long I could keep up. Then Larry broke into a run.

"Come on! They're gettin' away!" he shouted.

Somehow we followed him. The cornstalks stung my face. My heart pounded in my chest. Still we ran. Then, ahead of us, I could just see the outline of another fence. Suddenly, a pheasant exploded upward to my right. A gun sounded, and the bird came crashing down. Then another took to the air and another. Shotguns were cracking up and down our little line. Without warning, a big cock catapulted out of the grass at my feet. I brought the gun

BOB WHITE

to my shoulder and fired. The bird tumbled. A second cock came out of the cover on the left in front of Larry. When he was well out front, I swung on him. But a split second before I yanked the trigger, I heard a report and the bird fell.

It was over. The four of us stood there breathing hard, streams of sweat running down our faces. Larry was already on the other side of the fence, picking up pheasants. He held up what looked to be four or five cocks.

"I think we're gonna have to put a little more pep in it, fellers," he said.

Driving home that evening, we passed a group of attractive buildings just off the highway. Wood smoke curled warmly from the chimney of the largest one.

"What's that, Larry?" I asked.

"Oh, that's where them big city fellers from Sioux Falls come to hunt. I hear they got a regular full-time man there just to train them dogs. They say they bring a Frenchman all the way from Omaha to cook for them. I never heard of anything so silly. Have you fellers?"

I looked over at John. His face was pressed against the car window, his eyes wet with tears.

That night we fell into our bunks like Marine recruits in the first week of boot camp. The next day went much the same. We soon realized, with sinking hearts, there were to be no glimmering days trekking the rolling prairie, no matched pairs of blooded dogs, frozen one behind the other. No nights around the big stone fireplace in the lodge, sipping single malt whiskey and reliving the day's adventures.

The following day, we had lunch in the field. Larry passed out sandwiches. We still couldn't identify what was between those two slices of white bread. Behind Larry's back, George began to refer to it as Mystery Meat. The third day we were hunting a field close to home when a bird got up on my end. We watched it sail a good distance and land near a dilapidated barn.

"You ain't gonna let that sidewinder get away, are you?" Larry challenged. "Who's goin' after him?"

Everyone looked at me.

"Okay, I guess it *is* my bird," I said.

When I got to the barn, I walked around it carefully. Then I spotted him, a wily old pheasant rooster trotting along ahead of me well out of range. I increased my pace a little and tried to close the gap. But the faster I went, the faster he went. When I stopped, he stopped. When I rounded the barnyard at full gallop, he did too. I never gained an inch on him. Finally, in frustration, I did an about-face and took off around the barn the other way. I met him coming toward me. The poor old bird looked at me with an expression of astonishment. Due to his forward momentum, he had no way out but straight up. Unfortunately for him, he sailed right over my companions. George folded him like a dishcloth.

Driving home that evening, Larry was in a sanguine mood. "I got to admit it. That first day, I thought you fellers was a bunch of sissies. But, by golly, you turned out to be pheasant hunters after all."

The next morning we said good-bye in front of the farmhouse. Larry was clean-shaven and had on a spanking new ball cap. This one read "Farmers are Earthy." But there was something else different about him. At first, I couldn't put my finger on it. Then he smiled, exposing a set of snow-white choppers that would have made any movie actor envious. They were the size of Chiclets.

Ma insisted on giving everyone a hug. Then she presented each of us with a greasy paper bag containing a Mystery Meat sandwich. Larry shook hands all around. He seemed genuinely sad to see us go. I felt a little pang of remorse as we drove away. In spite of everything, we'd grown fond of the couple. I had no regrets. Maybe it wasn't pretty. Maybe we'd hunted pheasants like farm boys. But what the heck, we'd shot some birds.

The day after I returned home, I got a phone call. It was Hawkeye. He sounded like a different person. "Have you heard the news? I closed the Morris deal! It's the biggest sale in the history of the company! And the IRS has dropped the audit. Hawkeye's back, baby!"

"That's wonderful."

"By the way, how was the pheasant hunt? I hope I didn't miss much."

"You want the truth?"

"Of course."

"I'll never forget it as long as I live."

22

The Guided Duck Hunter

From *Shooting Sportsman*

"Holy John Browning !!!!!!" I yelped.I had been standing in the edge of the river, trying to pull our old johnboat off the trailer. The old tub had a way of sticking to the runners on cold mornings. That day she was stuck tighter than a seed tick. When she broke loose, she came at me like a runaway freight car. I stumbled backward, flailing my arms. Thankfully, by working an acre or so of river water into froth, I was able to stay on my feet. But the damage was done. Water had skimmed in over the top of my waders and soaked my long johns to the knees.

I sloshed ashore. I found my partner, the Deacon, howling and dancing around like a wounded Cossack.

"What is it?" I asked.

He held up one of the fingers on his right hand and winced. Somehow it had gotten caught in the winch.

"That looks pretty bad," I said. "Maybe we ought to put a bandage on that."

"Just a flesh wound," he said, gritting his teeth.

That was the Deacon for you, a real trouper. He never complained. And neither did I in those days. We were young and, in all modesty, in top physical and mental condition. To us, waterfowling was less a sport and more a test of stamina and endurance. One's place in the hierarchy of duck hunters depended on one's ability to withstand pain and torture. Both of us had experienced much worse things. A smashed finger or wet long johns were hardly worth consideration. And certainly they were no reason to cancel a hunt.

After a few minutes, the Deacon had recovered well enough to start loading his gear.

"Here, take this stuff," he said, opening the back end of his beat-up International Scout.

First, he passed me his old Browning humpback. Next came one blind bag, one case of 12 gauge ammo, a rain slicker, a bundle of camouflage netting, one jiggle duck, a folding lawn chair, a spool of twine, two dozen magnum decoys, a machete, a shovel, a hand saw, a pry bar, a claw hammer, a bucket of nails, a four-pack of toilet paper and a small pile of scrap lumber. Finally he opened the wire kennel in the back of the vehicle. Bo, the Deacon's old Lab, got to his feet and yawned. Then he jumped down, trotted over, and hopped into the boat, curling up in the last square foot of space.

"I hope you didn't bring much stuff," the Deacon said.

"Well, I guess I could leave most of mine here," I answered, making an attempt at sarcasm.

"Good idea," he said. "Let's get a move on."

I did manage to get my old Parker on board along with a handful of no. 4s. The Deacon climbed over the pile of lumber and squirmed into the back of the boat. He was much better with mechanical things than I. So I left the operation of the outboard to him. It was a system we had devised to best utilize each other's talents. Just as he was pulling the starter rope for about the 100th time, he stopped.

"Will you look at that!" he exclaimed in disgust.

"What?" I asked.

"Those guys over there," he said scornfully.

A big late model car had parked near the water, and three men in late middle age got out. Lit by the car's interior lights, they pulled on their heavy hunting coats, laughing and joking with each other. Then they walked the short distance to the boat dock, each carrying nothing more than a shotgun. A young hunting guide met them there. He greeted them with a cheerful "good morning" and helped them into the boat, cautioning each one to watch his step.

"What about them?" I asked.

"What about them?" the Deacon asked with astonishment. "Don't you see? They're guided duck hunters! Just look at them." He went on contemptuously, "They drive out here in a big, warm car and then walk twenty-five feet to a waiting boat. Then the guide takes them to the best blind on the lake where the decoys are already set out and the brushwork is already done. He helps them up the ladder. When the heater is started, and the blind is all warm and toasty, he serves them coffee and biscuits. That's just not duck hunting, not duck hunting at all."

We saw them sometimes at the sporting goods shop, those old geezers wearing silk neckties with mallards and pintails on them. They were usually talking about shooting here and shooting there with this guide or that guide and about how much fun they'd had. They were obviously not serious duck hunters because none of them had any visible wounds or scars. Anyway, the Deacon and I figured that we knew more about waterfowling than any guide living.

On the 135th pull, the old motor gave up and started. It sputtered, coughed, and put up a cloud of smoke as thick as the pyrotechnics at a rock concert.

"Okay, get in," the Deacon called out.

"Where?" I shouted. "I can't see a thing."

"Follow the sound of my voice!" he answered.

After stumbling around the landing for what seemed like a half hour and bumping into a very jumpy man from Georgia, I found the boat and got in. Or rather got on, since there was no place for me to sit except perched on top of the two bags of decoys. When the smoke cleared, I could see that we were riding pretty low in the water. There were no more than a couple of inches of freeboard between the top of the gunwale and the river.

Unperturbed, we set out through the darkness. Our blind was several miles away on a winding course through flooded timber and buck bushes. It wasn't unusual for us to take what we sometimes called the "long way" to the blind. And that morning was no exception. After a half hour, we found ourselves poking along an alley hemmed in by thick undergrowth. Finally, we were forced to stop. The boat was stuck in a tangle of vines and bushes. The temperature had dropped ten more degrees, and the wind was making weird howling noises through the trees. Then the batteries gave out on our only flashlight.

"Oh, well. Who needs a flashlight?" the Deacon said. "I can see fine."

"Me, too," I agreed.

"Yep, my eyes are already adjusting," he said as he twisted my ear, thinking it was the throttle on the outboard.

"Ouch!"

"And there's another thing I'm glad of," he announced.

"What's that?"

"I'm really glad we're not lost."

After taking a heretofore unknown route to the blind by way of Ohio, we finally arrived. When we'd put most of the gear inside, the Deacon began trying to coax old Bo up the ladder into the blind.

"Get up there, you old coward!" he shouted.

Since the Deacon and I had decided that I was the better carpenter, most of the blind building had been done by me. To the old dog, with his limited knowledge of construction, it probably looked like a lopsided child's playhouse. But once you learned where to step so as not to fall through the floor, there was nothing to be afraid of. After much whining and protest, Bo finally consented to go inside.

Then the Deacon tried to push him out the little front door and onto the dog stand. I suppose to Bo, the dog stand looked least sturdy of all. It was, after all, made up of some scraps I had left over after completing the blind. To the untutored eye, it probably resembled the Tower of Babel or maybe Pisa or maybe a Salvador Dali painting. But I thought Bo was being unreasonable. I've seen dogs in circuses sit on much smaller and shakier things and while balancing a ball on their noses. The Deacon pushed and shoved, but Bo wouldn't budge.

"You old chicken!" he grunted. "Get out there!"

Finally, with a mighty effort, the Deacon shouldered Bo through. Then, as quick as a flash, he slammed the little door shut, blocking Bo's return. The old dog whined and cried pitifully, but the Deacon wouldn't yield.

"I never thought I'd be saying this," he whispered, "but I think Bo's losing his nerve."

By the time we'd finished putting out the decoys, it was almost nine. The temperature continued to drop. The sky grew darker, and snowflakes swirled around in the treetops.

"How about a sip of that hot coffee?" I asked.

"Don't mind if I do," the Deacon said. "Pass it on down."

"Pass what down?"

"The hot coffee."

"But I don't have any coffee."

"Then why did you just offer me some?"

"I didn't."

"You distinctly said, 'How about a sip of hot coffee?'"

"But I only meant that I wanted some."

"I never suggested that you shouldn't have some!" he said irritably.

Just as I was about to reply, I realized that I had lost all feeling in my lower body. The water that had run down inside my waders had, by then, worked its way to my toes. What had begun as a stinging sensation had progressed to pain and then to the latter stages of hypothermia.

"I'll be darned if I'm not a bit chilly," I announced. "I think I'll fire up the old charcoal heater."

"I knew you were going to say that," the Deacon said.

"Why?"

"Because I didn't bring it," he answered.

"Why not?"

"Well, I can't think of everything! Anyway, only a guided duck hunter would need a heater on a nice day like this."

"On second thought, you're right," I said, my teeth chattering. "Who needs a heater?"

Then our pothole froze over. The ice had started around the edges and crept in toward the center until our decoys were mired in a translucent sheet.

"This is great! Mallards love weather like this!" the Deacon said. "I'll take the johnboat and bust out our shooting hole."

He made his way to the back of the blind. Then there was silence.

"Oh, boy. Now you've done it," he called out.

"Done what?"

"You forgot to tie up the johnboat. That's what."

I joined him at the rear of the blind and peeked over the edge. Sure enough, the johnboat was nowhere in sight. Then I saw that the frayed bowline was still tied securely to the blind. I followed it to its end.

"There she is," I said.

The old scow was right under our noses. It was sitting peacefully on the bottom under about five feet of icy water. Just then a big aluminum V hull came cruising up the river channel. It was the same boat we'd seen the guide take out early that morning. His clients, the three well-fed old relics, were seated comfortably in the forward seats. When they saw us, they waved happily. Then each one held up a limit of ducks, grinning and giving us the victory sign.

Gosh, I said, "They've already limited out, and they're going in."

"Pretend you don't see them," the Deacon said.

"Why?" I asked.

"Humph, guided duck hunters!" he snorted.

So the Deacon and I didn't wave back. We snubbed them. But they hardly seemed to notice the insult. The big boat continued on its way up the channel. As it disappeared around the bend, I could see the three beefy old fossils laughing and slapping each other on the back.

It is twenty-five years later. Dawn breaks crisp and cold over the river bottom. The first rays of sunlight filter through the bare sweet gums and pin oaks and sparkle on the water like jewels. There is an open pool in front of our blind, broken out before dawn, where our decoys bob in the fresh breeze.

"Two o'clock," Larry whispers, pointing to a spot somewhere out front.

I drop two steel no. 2s into my Parker reproduction and search the horizon. He puts the call to his mouth and starts the long paean of the highball. The birds waver, float on the air. They are undecided, tentative. Finally they move on.

"When the sun gets higher, those mallards are gonna start working" Larry says. "We limited out here yesterday by nine o'clock."

I pull the earflaps down on my fur cap and snuggle a little deeper into my hunting coat. It's a new one, a size or two larger than the last one. These modern coats aren't sized as accurately as the old ones.

"Warm enough, Mr. Bob?" Larry asks.

"Oh, yes, I'm fine."

"How about you, Mr. Maxwell?"

"I'm fine, Larry," the Deacon answers.

"Don't hesitate to tell me if you're uncomfortable. I can turn up the heater."

"No, no that's not necessary."

"More coffee?"

"I wouldn't mind," the Deacon says, taking the cup from him.

Then we sit for a long time without speaking, taking in this landscape with all our senses, this beautiful and mysterious place, this primeval expanse of water and hardwood. Finally I break the silence.

"Larry?"

"Yes, sir, Mr. Bob?"

"Got any more of those biscuits?"

23

Frozen

It's surprising what harrowing adventures a man will agree to undertake while standing in front of a warm fire in possession of a glass of red wine and a full stomach. Benny Goodwin and I had arrived in late afternoon at Deacon Maxwell's Arkansas duck camp. He greeted us at the front door.

"Come in, waterfowlers! Come in!" he shouted.

Mr. M. Porter Maxwell, or the Deacon, was a large man and dependably cheerful. He gave each of us a bear hug and a slap on the back that could have cleared an air passage. He was indeed a deacon at the First Presbyterian Church. But I'd never seen him display much religion ... except in the pursuit of waterfowl.

When Benny and I carried our duffels up the stairs and around the landing to our assigned room, I noticed that the beds in the other bedrooms were neatly made, and the rooms were absent of gear. It seemed we had the place to ourselves. At the time, I didn't attach much significance to the fact. We put our things away and went back downstairs.

The Deacon was standing behind the bar.

"Benny, Ranger Bob, step up here and wet your beaks!" he called out, holding up his glass. "The only thing better than duck hunting is duck hunting with fine old friends!" The Deacon always called me Ranger Bob.

As I said, our host was a jovial man. But that afternoon the Deacon seemed almost too jovial. Something about his demeanor lacked sincerity. Sure enough, halfway through our drink, his smile crumbled like a new bride's pie crust.

"Okay. I'll be honest, fellows," he said, "the hunting hasn't been very good the last week or so. In fact, ducks are as scarce around here as chicken lips."

He was referring to hunting out of his usual pit, the one he and his current partners leased every season. There were days when shooting that pit had been historic. But success in waterfowling is, as every veteran knows, uneven. After all, it was the end of the season. The whole countryside was iced over.

"But never fear!" the Deacon shouted bravely. "We'll give it hell in the morning!"

"You never know," Benny said. "The ducks might come back tomorrow."

"That's the spirit, Benny Boy!" our host declared.

He freshened our drinks and made another attempt at lightheartedness. But soon his smile sagged as he grew tired of the charade. About that time his cell phone went off.

"Hello. Oh, hi, Chris," he said. "I'm fine, Chris. Where, Chris? You think so, Chris? Great, Chris! I'll call you back, Chris!" He clicked off his phone. "That was Chris!" he affirmed as if Benny and I had not been standing three feet away. "And he's found some ducks!" The Deacon's mood had suddenly lifted. His voice grew a little louder. "Chris works for Curtis Nash, our landowner," he explained. "He says there are about a hundred mallards sitting on one of the reservoirs next to some flooded woods! There's a pool of open water!" He spread his arms wide as if displaying a pool.

"Great!" Benny said. "So there's a blind?"

"Well ... no," the Deacon answered.

"So we'll shoot out of a boat?"

"You can't get there in a boat."

"Then how do we ...?"

"We've got it all figured out!" the Deacon interrupted. "We'll put on our chest waders and wade in through the woods behind the reservoir, breaking a little ice of course. When we get to the edge of the lake, the ducks will take off. But that's okay. We'll throw out a few deeks and wait for them to come back. After all, everything else is frozen!"

"But there's no blind?" Benny asked.

"No problem!" the Deacon declared. "We can hide in the edge of the woods behind the trees!" He had grown more animated, dodging to one side and crouching down a little, like a man hiding behind a tree.

I knew our host as well as I knew the sight plane on my old Browning Auto.

When in pursuit of waterfowl, he was famously immune to suffering and cold.

"How far is it through those woods, Deacon?" I inquired.

"It's my understanding that it's about a hop and a skip!" he answered as cheerfully as a new schoolteacher.

"How far is that?"

"I'm told, maybe a jump and a leap!"

In spite of his merry assessment, I had reservations. "I'm not sure about this, Deacon," I said. "It's going to be as cold as a taxman's heart in the morning."

"Yeah," Benny agreed. "And the ice will be several inches thick."

"Hey, no problem," our host said without losing his smile. "Just thought I'd mention it. Anyway, we don't have to decide right now. Let's get some dinner!"

When we got back from the restaurant, we were all in a grand mood. There's nothing like a plate of deep fried Arkansas everything to put a man right with the world. The Deacon saw his opportunity. He reintroduced his proposal.

"I wish I could say I feel confident about shooting out of the pit tomorrow, fellows," he said, putting on a concerned face. "But I must admit that our prospects are poor. On the other hand, if we decide to follow Chris's plan, there might be a ..."

Now, before the glowing fire and with a full stomach, the proposition didn't sound so bad. In fact, for me, it had taken on a certain romance, an adventure, the makings of a tale. The warm fire was pleasant on my backside. I swirled the red wine in my glass. There was silence. The Deacon looked at me, then at Benny, then back at me.

We met Chris the next morning before dawn. He was a clean-cut young fellow, probably in his late twenties, the kind of upstanding young citizen that Arkansas seems to raise in abundance. He was landowner Curtis Nash's right-hand man, his protégé, and was being taught the difficult science of making farming pay in the twenty-first century. Chris already knew the Deacon well. After introductions, I became "Mr. Bob" and Benny became "Mr. Benny." This was the South, after all. When I passed the sixty mark, I began being addressed that way. I finally gave up my vanity and accepted it.

"We'll use my truck," Chris said. "Let's pile in."

Benny and I took the backseat. After a short and muddy ride, we stopped atop a wide levee. The four of us got out and began pulling on our chest waders. The woods at the bottom of the incline looked black and impenetrable.

Owing to Chris's age, no one objected when he took the lead. He waded in, breaking ice with the butt of his shotgun and pushing aside vines and buck bushes. The Deacon followed, manning the flashlight. I was next in line, and Benny was in the rear. The trees were huge, and there were ropy vines winding up into the canopy. In summer, it would have been good place to make a Tarzan movie. Twenty or thirty feet in, I noticed the water was only a few inches below the top of my chest waders. Hidden logs and branches made each step precarious. In some places, we had no choice but to use our gun straps and clasp hands to keep our footing. After what seemed like miles, we reached the edge of the reservoir. The ducks were there all right. They took flight and sailed out over the fields, the susies putting up a racket. In the pool in front of us little waves chopped the surface. The rest of the reservoir was frozen in a thick sheet of ice, as motionless as a photograph. Chris threw out our half dozen deeks.

I started toward a likely looking hiding place and just then felt an unpleasant sensation under the arch of my right foot. Then it began creeping out-

ISTOCK

ward. It was water. Somewhere during the course of our trek, I had punched a hole in my right wader. In subfreezing temperatures, this was disastrous. I found a position between two trees and propped my right boot against one, out of the water. But the damage was done. My foot was soaked. It began to grow numb. I knew I couldn't make it back through the woods alone. Neither could I go forward around the edge of the reservoir through the ice without help. And calling an early end to the hunt would ruin it for everyone else, especially after all we'd been through to get there. I had no choice but to tough it out. As we waited, time moved like a glacier. I was cold. My mind drifted.

It was the tail end of an especially severe winter. At the Old River Rod and Gun, Bloody Mary Society and Gentlemen's Club, where the Deacon and I had been members for decades, the hunting had been excellent that season. But in late January, temperatures dipped to record lows, and everything froze as hard as granite. No ducks had been seen in at least a week. In spite of it all, the Deacon shamed me into rolling out of my warm bunk at 5:30 a.m. and making the bitter hike to old No. 7. We left three other members behind, warm in their bunks. They refused to get up.

"Bunch of sissies," the Deacon mumbled as we made our way up the levee.

Two weeks before, the Deacon and I had discovered an unfrozen pool at field No. 5 and splashed two limits of green heads and widgeons before the sun was well up. But two weeks had passed since then.

No. 7 faces north. There was a fierce wind blowing. When I peeked over the front edge of the blind, it felt like being hit with birdshot. I would later learn that it was seventeen below zero that morning. We managed to get a fire started in our little charcoal heater, even though it did little good. A field mouse had made a home under the heater, and the noise drove him out. He scampered up the front wall of the blind. When he reached the top and the wind struck him, he froze as stiff as a top hat. I picked up the little fellow by the tail and put him near the heater. It was too late.

"It's a sign from God, Deacon," I said.

"But, Ranger Bob, we can't leave now! Mallards fly late on mornings like this!"

"*You* wait for them," I replied.

You're awfully quiet over there, Ranger," the Deacon said, bringing me back to the present.

"I was in meditation," I answered. "I've taken up Zen."

"The hell you have!" he said. "Listen, Chris seems to thinks those ducks aren't coming back!"

"Oh?"

I could tell Chris and Benny were uncomfortable. After all, they were standing waist deep in ice water. The Deacon was another matter. He looked as cozy as a dog on a heat grate.

"What do *you* think, Benny?" he asked, hoping Benny would want to stay.

"Well ..."

I waited, holding my breath. My right foot throbbed.

"I say let's punt," Benny said.

Yes! Thank you, Benny. I thought.

"I think he's right Mr. Porter," Chris said. "We may as well go."

"How about you, Ranger?" the Deacon asked hopefully.

"Well, if you fellows want to quit, I'm fine with that," I said, my teeth chattering.

The Deacon had no choice but to yield. Chris gathered the decoys, and we started out, not back through the woods but around the edge of the reservoir. It appeared easier. The Deacon took the lead, claiming he had devised a "better method of breaking ice." Every few steps he placed our bag of decoys on top of the ice and pushed down until it broke, then he moved forward. It was slow going. Benny was growing impatient. He worked his way to the front.

"I'll take over, Deacon," he said.

Off he went, stomping through the ice, goose-stepping like one of Hitler's storm troopers. Four or five yards farther, he went down like a bowling pin. He crashed through the ice and disappeared. A second later he surfaced. "Log! Underwater!" he sputtered. He was soaked head to foot.

I took the lead from Benny and soon stepped in a hole. Freezing water came in over the top of my waders, adding to my misery. Chris got in front again. We trudged after him as best we could.

Finally we reached the levee and clambered to the top. It was about fifty yards to where we'd left the vehicle. Benny and I took off in a clumsy lope, hampered by waders and gear. When we reached the SUV, we got in and started shucking layers of icy wet clothing. Chris and the Deacon arrived a moment later.

"The heater, Chris! The heater!" we shouted.

That evening, back at the Deacon's camp house, we sat in front of a crackling fire discussing the day's events. After our customary breakfast and afternoon nap, the morning's debacle had begun retreating into memory. My recollection of the cold and misery we'd suffered was beginning to sting less, as things do when viewed through the prism of time ... and comfort.

"I apologize, fellows," the Deacon said. "I should never have led you on that awful trek this morning. To make up for it, I promise to take you to the pit tomorrow, ducks or no ducks. We'll be as warm and dry as rabbits in a burrow. I'll bring hot coffee, doughnuts, sausage, and biscuits. You'll think you're at the Peabody Hotel!"

Just then he put his phone to his ear. "Oh, hi, Chris. Really, Chris! Where, Chris?"

24

Laissez Les Bon Temps Rouler

Letting the good times roll at Live Oak

"Wait a minute, Deacon."

"What for?"

"You'll see. Don't start yet."

We sat in our rented car outside the lodge at Live Oak Plantation. In the early morning darkness, I turned the dial on the car radio, moving past static and distant voices. The Deacon drummed his fingers on the car steering wheel.

We sat in our rented car outside the lodge at Live Oak Plantation. In the early morning darkness, I turned the dial on the car radio, moving past static and distant voices. The Deacon drummed his fingers on the car steering wheel.

"Come on, Bob, it'll be light soon."

"One more minute."

Then I found it. It came streaming across the airwaves like a ghost from some antique gramophone.

"Jolie blonde, regardez donc quoi t'as fait
Tu m'as quitte pour t'en aller"

The singer belted out the pain of lost love, the pretty blonde who'd gone home to her family. The accordion pumped the waltz time. I'd hit the jackpot. Not only had I found an all-French station, we were listening to "Jolie Blonde," the Cajun national anthem.

"Now we can go," I announced.

"You're crazy," the Deacon said, grinning.

He put the car in gear, and we pulled away from the lodge under the giant live oak tree and out onto the road that leads to the levees. Along with a half dozen other friends, we'd been invited to spend a weekend of waterfowling and revelry at Live Oak Plantation, a private hunting and fishing preserve in

South Louisiana. Live Oak has belonged to the same Louisiana family for a hundred years.

"Jolie Bloooooonde!" I warbled, singing along with the radio.

"You're going to scare the ducks," my partner said.

I could sense that the Deacon's focus was narrowing. The closer we got to our blind, the more serious he became.

"What time did everyone get to bed last night?" he asked.

"I don't know. Not late," I said.

"Did you get enough sleep?"

"Of course," I said defensively.

"Duck hunting is a contest of wits between man and nature, Bob. And nature always gets a good night's sleep."

"I know, Deacon," I yawned.

I'd heard that adage a dozen times. Mr. M. Porter Maxwell, the Deacon, was no teetotaler and certainly no prude. But as far as he was concerned, we had come to Louisiana to hunt ducks. If it had been up to him, he would have closed the bar and declared lights out at nine.

The afternoon before, we rehearsed the drive to our blind. Now, in the pre-dawn darkness, we were traveling by memory. All that was visible in the headlights was the road atop the narrow levee ahead. But we knew what lay on each side: shallow coastal marshes stretching away to the gulf, crawfish traps poking above the water, and sleeping alligators.

"This is it," the Deacon said, pulling to the edge of the levee.

We slipped our shotguns and blind bags off the backseat and walked the few steps to the water's edge. Our boat was tied up and waiting for us. It was a dainty little craft, vaguely shaped like a canoe, but with a flat bottom and about a third the draft. At the stern was a flat area, just big enough for one man to stand. The boat is called a pirogue. And it is said that one can "float on a dew drop." The little vessel is not meant to be propelled by a paddle or outboard motor, indeed no motors are allowed at Live Oak. It is poled in the old tradition by a man standing at the stern.

Since the Deacon claimed that he had poled a pirogue once or twice before, I had no choice but to trust our lives, shotguns, and gear to him. I crawled to the front of the little vessel.

"One thing, Bob," he said.

"What?"

"Pretend you're a sack of potatoes."

"Why?"

"That's what they say down here. It means be perfectly still. So pretend you're a sack of potatoes."

"Sack of potatoes it is," I said, holding onto the sides.

Live Oak lies in the heart of Cajun country. The Cajuns arrived in Louisiana in the 1740s after being pushed out of what is now Nova Scotia by the British. The Spanish government of Louisiana at the time took many of these French-speaking exiles in, granting each family, along with land, an ax, a hoe, a sickle, a spade, two hens, a cock, and a month-old pig. The head of every family also received a shotgun. That shotgun would prove to be a valuable asset since the area teemed with ducks, geese, and other game birds. The Cajuns carved out livelihoods as small farmers, fur trappers, and fishermen. But later, many became market hunters, supplying the restaurants and butcher shops of the period with waterfowl. Lake Arthur, on the coast south of Live Oak, was once considered the market-hunting capitol of the world. That practice was stopped, or at least declared illegal, at the end of World War I.

We arrived at our assigned mound of earth unscathed. I was impressed with my partner's skill with the pirogue. I even considered complimenting him but ... naaaah.

Buried in the center of our little island, a few feet apart, were two round plastic sink cans or cylinders. When we pulled off the tops, neither of us stepped down inside. We were told that water moccasins sometimes found their way into these cans. As my flashlight lit the bottom of each one, I felt myself recoil involuntarily. I'll admit it; I'm scared of snakes. It goes beyond a healthy, well-informed fear. I'm scared of the damned things. One water moccasin bite is recorded in the logs at Live Oak. I don't remember if the victim died or not.

The Deacon and I climbed in and loaded up just as the first hint of morning lit up our decoys. We'd brought our "meat guns," heavy American autos suited for the vast marshes of the New World.

"Good Lord, look at this scenery," I whispered. "This is spectac ..."

"Shoot!" he yelled, making me almost clear the top of my sink box.

A half dozen teal had slipped in behind us. They sailed away over our spread full throttle. Each of us sent a wasted pattern at their hind ends. Teal often fly at sunrise, and these were right on schedule. Soon they were buzzing us like Zeros.

"On your side, Bob!"
"Behind you, Deacon!"
"Get him!"
"Good shot!"
"Coming in!"
"Out front!"
"He's yours!"
"Damn! That was a little close to my ear, Bob!"
"I'm sorry, Deacon."
"What?"
"I'm sorry."
"What?"
"Never mind."

The Deacon and I often bickered over the fine points of poaching on each other's shooting space. He was right. I had erred. But my partner had blasted my ears often enough. I'd learned to wear my earplugs and to put them in there as tight as a cork in a wine bottle.

The water was, of course, still. There was no need to rush out and pick up a dead bird. They weren't going anywhere. When we'd downed five each (the number of shells fired will go unreported), we waded out to retrieve our ducks. Retrievers are not often used in South Louisiana, especially in warm weather. A swimming dog looks much like a nutria, a large fur-bearing rodent. And to an alligator, a nutria is groceries.

Finally, my partner romanced a couple of green heads into our decoys like a Siren calling Ulysses' sailors. We had limited out. The Deacon was ecstatic. He pumped my hand, then slapped me on the back so hard you'd have thought I was choking on a ham sandwich.

"It's been a story book morning, my friend!" he shouted. "Absolutely story book!"

It was the Deacon's phrase for a perfect hunt, *story book*, the primary prerequisite being shooting a limit. If we had been one duck short, it wouldn't have been story book. I began packing up.

"What's the hurry?" he asked. "It's early. We could watch the birds for a few minutes."

"I know but remember, they said they'd come out and check on us at 8:30. We don't want them to worry."

"Oh, yes. They might think we've been eaten by a ... well, you know."

ISTOCK

There is no afternoon shooting in the marshes at Live Oak. If pressured too much, the ducks will move out. However, young, energetic teenagers sometimes spend afternoons in the fields trying to sneak snow geese. I didn't join them. I'm hardly a teenager. Furthermore, I spent enough time during my boyhood on the coast of Texas crawling snow geese. A snow goose's eyesight is as sharp as a country boy's pocketknife. A crawler rarely succeeds.

That evening we were treated to *the* classic Louisiana dinner, a crawfish boil. Crayfish, crawdads, mudbugs, it's all the same delicious little crustacean. The kitchen cooks prepared the side dishes, but our host did up the crawfish himself. He huddled over the big cauldron on the front porch like a Shakespearean conjurer. The pot was the size of a bathtub and fired with propane. When the little critters were pinkish-red, he dipped them out into buckets. In the dining room, the long table had been laid end to end with butcher's paper. At the opportune moment, he slung a bucket of crawfish down the length of the table, then another from the other end. Not one hit the floor. Each diner was expected to stand tableside and peel his own dinner. The cooks brought out corn on the cob and little boiled potatoes.

After dinner, port and sherry were brought out. The Deacon immediately stood up and made a great show of stretching and yawning.

"It seems to me that all good waterfowlers ought to be in bed about now," he said.

Nobody moved. He looked me directly in the eye like some mountain preacher about to cast out a demon. "Duck hunting is a contest of wits between man and nature," he began, and nature always ..."

"I'll be along in a few minutes, Deacon," I said.

"Okay," he said, not quite sure I could be trusted. Then he headed toward the bedrooms.

The next morning we got lost. We weren't *lost* lost because we knew we'd be able to eyeball the levee when the sun came up. But we didn't find our sink boxes until late. Then the Deacon's shotgun failed. He was digging spent shells out of it with a nail clipper. We finished with only three birds each. My partner was sullen. He hardly said a word on the way back to the lodge. Not limiting out was, to him, a sin against waterfowling or perhaps an admission of second-rate skills.

"I wonder if anybody else shot a limit?" he said with a worried look.

After lunch, I proposed that we ride out to the levees and look at the marsh.

"No. I'd better rest up and clean the old auto," he answered. "We've got to be sharp tomorrow. I don't want a repeat of what happened this morning."

Asking the Deacon to take his eyes off the prize was like expecting a cobra to ignore a flute. When I walked through the lodge, it appeared the whole household had decided on a nap. I drove back to the levee alone. The sun had popped out, and the temperature had risen into the high fifties. I stopped the car and slipped on my hip waders. The pirogue was just where we'd tied it that morning.

If you get wet, it's not like you're going to freeze to death, I told myself.

About fifty yards away, a small alligator slid off a shallow mud bank into the water. Carefully, I crawled onto the back end of the little boat. Then, using the pole to keep my balance, I stood up. I took a deep breath and pushed the pirogue forward. It trembled and moved out into the water. I realized that the pole was not only for propulsion. The marsh floor was firm enough to steady me. After each push, I only needed to be centered and dead still. *You're doing fine,* I thought. *Sack of potatoes. Sack of potatoes.* The afternoon had turned beautiful. Another evening of fun and Cajun food awaited me and another morning of duck shooting. I was all alone and suddenly overcome with happiness. I couldn't help myself.

"Jolie Bloooooonde!"

During the last few years storms have racked the Gulf Coast. Live Oak has not been spared. Hurricane Rita brought a seven-foot flood, inundating every building on the property. At the main lodge, only the upstairs survived untouched. Recently, all the structures have been rebuilt on seven- to eight-foot pilings. The marshes have begun to recover, but the extent of the environmental damage will not be known for years, perhaps decades. Alligators, however, are more plentiful than ever.

25

Marching with Napoleon

If someone told me the tale I'm about to tell you, I wouldn't believe it. So I won't blame you if *you* don't believe it. There are certain things a man will accept as truth on the basis of someone else's word and certain things he won't, pigs flying, for example. That's something I wouldn't believe simply on another person's testimony. I'd have to *see* a pig fly.

I arrived in late afternoon at K and M Hunting, near Plankinton, South Dakota, just in time to join the last pheasant drive of the day. After I put my gear away in the bunkhouse, one of the young guides drove me out to the field. My friend George Payne had hosted this hunt every year for a decade, and this year I was the new addition. I didn't know what to expect. We joined a group of men gathered at the rear of what appeared to be a repainted and refitted UPS van. I greeted George and Buddy Vaughn, the only two people in the gathering I knew.

"Bob," George said, "this is Michael Miller. He runs this circus." A large man with a bushy black beard stepped forward and offered me a big meaty hand.

"You bring a shotgun with you, Mr. Bob?" he asked.

"Yes, I did."

"Can you hit anything with it?"

"Well, sometimes."

"Good, you're just the man this bunch has been looking for." There were a few chuckles but mostly loud groans.

With Michael taking the center, we lined up across the edge of a field of stubble. The other two guides were his son, Levi, and Ryan, another local youth. All three were working big black Labs, which began quartering a short distance in front of us. There were ten shooters in our line, including the two flankers on the ends who were positioned about twenty yards ahead. At the far boundary of the cornfield, I could just see three blockers waiting. After a dozen steps, the first pheasant shot up like a bottle rocket. It was a little undersized, with short tail feathers and drab coloring. The shotgunners nearest to it hesitated, probably thinking it was a hen.

"Roosterrrr!" Michael yelled. No one fired. "Rooster, shoot the damn thing!" he shouted.

By then the bird was out of range of the line. It caught the wind and banked sideways. In half a second, it was already at the edge of the field streaking toward the tree line. I watched as a flanker put his shotgun to his shoulder and swung through. The gun jarred and the pheasant nose-dived.

"Get him, Lucky," Levi shouted, sending his Lab after the downed bird.

Levi was an exact duplicate of Michael, plus an inch or two. He also sported a black beard, though his was thinner in places. When his dog returned, he put the bird in his game pouch. Then he looked at Michael, waiting for the signal to start forward. But Michael had squatted down on his haunches and was peering ahead through the cornstalks. Then he stood up and looked behind him. Finally, he raised himself up on his toes and surveyed the edges of the field.

"Has anybody seen Napoleon?" he called out.

"He's not down here," someone answered.

"Haven't seen him," Brian said.

Just then a barrel-chested little Jack Russell terrier appeared. He was small, even by terrier standards, hardly a foot high. From his muscular chest, his body tapered rearward to a pair of undersized hips and spindly back legs.

"Here he is!" Michael shouted. The little dog came toward him. The rear of his body followed the front with a hopping motion, one back leg held up, inert. "The little bugger looks tired. I think I'll give him a ride," Michael said. He picked up the dog and stuffed him behind him into his game pouch. Napoleon squirmed around and poked his head out so that he could see over Michael's shoulder and get a clear view of the field. Ten feet farther in, the Labs put up another pheasant.

"Roosterrrr! Brian shouted as a big cock exploded skyward.

This one was a grown-up with long tail feathers and bright iridescent coloring. There were two reports. The first shot missed cleanly. But a second, from somewhere down the line, took the bird down. We moved forward. The last thing I wanted to do was poach a bird and make a bad first impression. Finally, I bagged a cock straight out. Buddy and George were shooting well, and our count mounted. I glanced over at Michael. Napoleon was riding along behind him like a papoose with what appeared to be an expression of approval.

When we reached the end of the field, the blockers moved out from under the trees and started toward us. We pushed the line forward slowly, forming a ring. Birds still on the ground were now surrounded. This last chapter of a pheasant drive is sometimes half humorously called the "circle of death." The phrase obviously refers to the death of pheasants. But I never look for a rising bird. I look at the men in the circle opposite me. In a microsecond, I was ready to kiss the earth like a returning astronaut. One bird went up like it had been shot out of a cannon. Thankfully these guys knew what they were doing. All but one of us held our fire. The drive was over. We gathered in a grassy strip at the end of the field.

The other van was waiting. It appeared to be a converted bread truck with benches added in the back for seating. On the way back to the barn, Napoleon rode in the back with the men, not in the kennel truck with the other dogs. He hopped up and down the little aisle between the benches, the center of attention. Each hunter and guide reached out affectionately to stroke his ears or pat his head. I sat across from Michael. To be heard over the noise of the truck, I had to shout, "So, what happened to Napoleon's back legs?"

"It's some kind of hip problem that he came down with a couple of years ago," he said. "The vet can't do much for him."

"That's too bad. Is it getting worse?"

"Oh, no. He's getting better," he said, brightening. "Last year this time he couldn't use his back legs at all."

I could imagine the little dog immobilized. I visualized him confined to his kennel or being carried around by someone. Or maybe they'd strapped a little cart to his hind end. I once saw such a thing.

"I guess you had to carry him around," I said.

"Oh, gosh, no. He just held his back end up in the air and walked on his front legs," Michael answered.

"What?"

"Yeah. Just walked on his front paws."

By then we had reached the barnyard.

Michael's wife, Kathy, and her helpers, put on a delicious dinner that evening. But all through it I couldn't stop thinking about Napoleon. A Jack Russell terrier trotting around the farm balanced on his front legs like a sidewalk acrobat. I wasn't sure I believed it. The tale might be a South Dakotan's idea of humor. Maybe it was a prank he and the guides and the veteran hunters pulled on the new man.

After dinner, I made friends with a few cigar smokers and side-by-side fanatics. We staked out an area in front of the bunkhouse to indulge our weaknesses. I broached the subject of Napoleon with one of the veterans.

"Oh, yeah," he testified, "I've seen him do it."

The next morning, on the way to the field, I started asking Michael more questions.

"So, does Napoleon really ... uh, hunt?"

"Of course. He's a good pheasant dog," he said. "And he's especially good at finding cripples."

"But he's so small?" I asked.

"Well, yes. One time I saw a big rooster drag him twenty yards."

I could understand that.

"But I've got to ask," I said. "How did you end up pheasant hunting with a Jack Russell terrier?"

"Well, I bought him to keep rats out of the barn. But Napoleon just wouldn't be left behind. Every time we loaded up to go hunting, he tried to get in the truck with us. So we gave up and let him come long. That was before his

ISTOCK

back legs got bad. First thing you know, he's out in front of the line quartering with the big dogs."

"He just picked it up?"

"Yep. Just picked it up."

"So he turned out to be a great asset in the field, huh?"

"Well, sort of. He's bad about starting fights with the other dogs."

"But he's so little."

"Yeah. But I don't think he knows it. I suspect that when Napoleon looks in the mirror, a big black dog looks back."

The last morning was clear and winter blue, a perfect day for sport. We climbed out of the van and started fanning out along a grassy road. The cornfield in front of us looked like it went on forever. Our three big Labs were bouncing around like kids on Christmas morning. Napoleon looked eager and happy. He had all four feet on the ground, even though one of his back legs was held a little tentatively. We started the line forward. Unlike the other dogs, no one "worked" Napoleon. He could freelance.

The dogs seemed to put up a bird every ten or twenty yards. By the time we reached the end, we must have had a dozen in hand. Then a final cock rose far out front. He was too far out for a sure kill. But when he reached the top of his trajectory and was about to veer sideways, several shooters pulled the trigger on him. The first two gunners missed. The third one got a pellet or two in him. He was, as the Brits say, "pricked." He sailed out over the cornstalks like a B17, too far ahead of even the flanker. I watched him glide into the distance and disappear in the tree line.

"You'll never get that bird," Levi called out.

"I suppose not," Michael said. "He'll make some varmint's dinner tonight."

"No bird, Lucky!" Levi shouted, calling back his dog.

We moved ahead, closing the ring. A final pheasant came up and was shot cleanly by one of the blockers. The van was waiting for us. I dug into the big cooler on the back, found a bottle of cold water, and sat down on the back bumper. Michael began kidding one of the younger men about his shooting. He took off the man's glasses and wiped them grandly with a large red bandanna, while the rest of the group looked on and laughed. The young man laughed too, seeming to enjoy it.

Just then, Brian shouted, "Hey, look!"

From the direction of the tree line, a big cock pheasant appeared to be walking, or rather floating toward us. At least that's how it looked at first. As it got closer, we could see that the bird was not walking at all. It was the crippled pheasant. He was being carried by Napoleon, whose little body was all but invisible behind the bird. Several of the men cheered.

That evening, a group of us were waiting in front of the bunkhouse when word came that dinner was ready. I was just about to start for the main house when I spotted Napoleon. He was making his way slowly down the stairs from the landing, one step at a time. He looked tired. When his front feet reached the ground, he hesitated, his back legs still on the bottom rung. Then he hiked his rear end in the air and walked across the barnyard on his front paws.

Kathy and her kitchen helpers put on a grand feast that night. There was pheasant prepared three ways, a smorgasbord of vegetables and side dishes, and finally rhubarb pie. I would have sworn the rhubarb pie was sweet potato, but these westerners set me straight. Kathy ran the table like a society matron hosting an embassy dinner party. She was a masterful hostess. As we left the main house, she called out behind us, "Now you fellows don't let Napoleon in the bunkhouse. He likes to sleep in there. But we'd prefer he slept out in the kennel with the other dogs."

An hour later, I said good night to the "cigar club" and went up the stairs to the landing. Napoleon was waiting by the door. Carefully putting myself between him and the doorway, I opened it slightly and started to squeeze through. But he was ready. He went around my feet and dashed inside quicker than a wind-up mouse. When I got inside, I looked up and down the long bunkroom. He was nowhere in sight. I pulled my duffel out from under my bunk to retrieve my shaving kit. I'd left the bag unzipped down the middle. Nestled in the center of it was Napoleon, curled up on one of my flannel shirts. He looked up at me sheepishly.

"You're supposed to sleep in the kennel with the other dogs, my friend," I said.

I reached down to pick him up, and like a flash, he scurried under the next bunk. I got down on my hands and knees and looked for him. He'd disappeared. I glanced around the room. It was a jungle of gun cases, luggage, extra gear, and dirty clothes. Somewhere, Napoleon was hiding, curled up in another warm spot. Perhaps his eyelids were already drooping. I knew I'd never find him. I took my toothbrush and headed for the bathroom. *To hell with it,* I thought. *Bonaparte never quartered with the troops either.*

26

How Not to Cook a Wild Duck

I stood fourth in line outside Bad Bob's Superior Duck Plucking Service in Brinkley, Arkansas. The morning's hunt had afforded me two mallards, a widgeon and a gadwall. My partners, Deacon Maxwell and Dr. John Farringer, stood in line behind me with their birds. For three dollars, Bad Bob and Co. were about to turn each of our ducks into a cleanly plucked, eviscerated fowl wrapped in butcher paper and hard frozen for the journey home. The young man in front of me struck up a conversation.

"Where do you fellows hunt?" he asked.

"We lease a field from a local family," I replied.

He volunteered that he and his partner had gone out with a guide that morning but had only bagged two ducks. He seemed to want to keep the conversation going. "We don't keep ours," he said.

"Keep what?"

"Our ducks. We don't keep them. I give mine to the maid."

"Why?"

"Well, they're really not very good, are they?"

There it was. I hadn't heard that said in a long time, but I knew there were still those out there who hadn't yet learned the secret of roasting waterfowl and who might still be victims of the aversion many of our mothers and grandmothers (mine included) had to serving rare meat, especially fowl. I didn't need to know the ugly details. But I asked anyway. "So you've tried cooking wild duck?"

"Oh, yes."

"How did you cook them?"

"Well, the first time my wife and I tried a recipe we found for duck with orange sauce. I think we roasted the duck an hour or so in the oven."

"And?"

"Well, you know. It was tough and tasted sort of like beef liver."

And so, as I am prone to do, I delivered my sermon like a downtown Methodist or Baptist preacher, quietly and in measured tones, but with conviction, "Young man, you cannot take a recipe from an ordinary kitchen cookbook and expect to have success with wild duck. Those recipes are to be used with fattened, pen-raised poultry farm birds. And don't be fooled if the recipe has the word *wild* in it. Look at the list of ingredients. If it begins with a 3 1/2 to 5-pound duckling, that means a supermarket duck. If you roast a smaller, leaner wild duck for an hour in the oven, it's going to be inedible. It needs to be cooked hot and fast and served medium rare."

He went away a wiser if somewhat browbeaten young man.

Any duck, wild or domestic for that matter, is tastier when served medium rare. Unlike turkey and chicken, duck is red meat and benefits from less cooking. Of course there is the concern about foodborne illnesses connected to undercooked fowl. But while the USDA recommends that all poultry be cooked to an internal temperature of 160 degrees, which is cooked through, pathogens such as salmonella are scarce in domestic duck and even scarcer in wild duck.

As far as my comment about ordinary kitchen cookbooks, meaning the ones not intended for game cooks, there are exceptions. One is that old standby, *The Joy of Cooking*. Irma Rombauer, the original author, grew up on Maryland's Eastern Shore in the early part of the last century in a family of hunters, and knew all about wildfowl. "Ideally," she said, "the juices are red and flow freely when the duck is carved." I like mine slightly more done than that, but not by much. The great cook and food writer, James Beard, in *Beard on Birds* agrees on the "red juices" and recommends roasting a wild duck only twenty minutes in a 500-degree oven.

For my taste, the best method is to start with a whole plucked bird, skin on. Rub the body with butter, and sprinkle salt and pepper all over, including in the cavity. Lay two small pieces of bacon across the breast. Place the bird breast up on a very hot gas or charcoal grill and cover. The drippings from the bacon may flame up, so you'll want to keep a water mister handy. Twenty minutes will do it for a large duck like a mallard. Smaller ducks will, of course, take less time. A very hot grill would approximate Mr. Beard's recommended 500-degree oven, and the cooking time would be the same, twenty minutes. Remove the cover, and check the doneness by slicing down the breast bone. Some bright red at the center is best. The more faint-hearted may want to cook it a little longer until the meat is deep pink. An internal temperature of 115 indicates medium rare. At my hunting club, those crispy legs are gnawed after dinner while the dishes are being washed. If you are roasting your whole duck indoors in the oven, do not place bacon across the breast. The hot bacon grease dripping onto a 500-degree pan underneath will put up enough smoke to set off your alarms and send you outdoors.

If you're not near a duck-plucker and you're not up to the tedium of plucking the bird yourself, you may want to breast it, that is, carve out the breast. Most of the meat is in the breast, so you won't lose much. The breast can be coated with a rub or marinated for an hour or so in a mixture of melted butter, Worcestershire sauce, and crushed garlic. Then it should be either grilled or sautéed to rareness. You'll want to carve the breast into medallions for the presentation. Medium rare wild duck tastes a little like beef tenderloin with some of that delicious gaminess that hunters and connoisseurs love.

There's also the cook-till-the-flesh-falls-off-the-bone method. I'm not a fan of it. There are many recipes for gumbos, stews, etc. that call for boiling the duck meat two hours before adding it to the pot. I'm sure it's tender by then, but it can hardly taste good. Duck gumbos or stews are wonderful the first day if the duck has been cooked properly, that is rare, cut up, and put in just before the dish is served. The problem is, if it's reheated later, the duck gets cooked through and then it tastes like, you know ... tough beef liver.

Dozens of sauces go well with wild duck, many of them exclusively for that purpose: juniper sauce, Col. Hawker sauce, the classic port wine reduction, and easy to make fruit-based sauces like plum or currant. If you don't want to go to the trouble of making a sauce, creamy horseradish sauce or chutney goes great with duck, right out of the jar.

When I was a boy, my mother ruined every wild duck I brought home. She was a fine southern cook but simply refused to serve rare fowl. Once, after I was grown, she was reminiscing about her beloved father, my grandfather, who died before I was born, and the fact that he was an avid duck hunter.

"So did Mamaw (my grandmother) cook them?" I asked.

"Oh, yes."

"What did they taste like?"

She thought this over for a moment, then answered, "Sort of like tough beef liver."

PART THREE

Way Far

27

Less Than the Best

From *Shooting Sportsman*

"Now, sir!" Brian shouted.

The two grouse, rocketing directly toward us, looked to be about seventy-five yards away, still well out of range. But my loader, Brian Robinson, knew his stuff. He was a ruddy-cheeked Yorkshireman who'd probably seen more grouse drives than King Edward VII. If he said shoot, who was I to disagree?

I pointed at the bird on the left and squeezed the trigger. It fell. Then I realized it had fallen within range. In the amount of time it had taken me to mount the gun and fire, the bird had traveled perhaps thirty-five yards.

"And again," he commanded.

The other bird sensed our presence in the butt, gained altitude, and shot over the top. I wasn't ready. I pulled hard but probably trailed him by several feet.

"And now behind," Brian barked, passing me the loaded gun on the inside and taking its empty mate on the outside. Two more grouse had slipped between our butt and the one next door, hugging the terrain, barely four feet above the heather. I swung past the first one and felt the gun's recoil as it tumbled. Swinging hard again, I sent a wasted shot after the second. By then it was far out of range.

"In front now, sir," Brian shouted.

My heart was pounding. Adrenaline was running through my blood like rocket fuel. Still I couldn't get my mind and body to match the speed of these birds.

Faster, I told myself. *You're still too slow.*

I missed my next shot out front but was able to take one in a group of three as they sailed over us. We were at the far end of the line with no gun on our right. A pair of birds suddenly appeared there, seeming to come out of nowhere. Without consciously mounting the gun or thinking, I pushed the barrels hard past the second bird. In the space of a fraction of a second, "the picture" appeared in my mind. But it was enough. At that instant the front bead was precisely the right distance ahead of it, the barrels were swinging at exactly the proper speed. I didn't consciously pull the trigger. I only felt the recoil and saw the grouse tumble.

"Four down, sir," Brian said. He seemed pleased in spite of all my misses. "They're quite fast today," he added. "There's a stiff wind behind them."

"Quite fast" was an understatement. I was reminded of what a friend of mine often said about teal: "Sit tight, fellows. If the world really is round, they'll be back in fifteen minutes."

Suddenly another pair was on us. They emerged from a low saddle in the hillside ahead, as if fired from a cannon. They zoomed skyward as they approached, sensing our presence. Pulling as hard as I could on the first one, I blotted him out and jerked the trigger. I had no idea if I'd hit him. Then I turned and sent the second one into the heather just behind me.

The beaters were closer now. They were stretched evenly across the horizon like the first line of a slow-moving infantry charge. The faint sound of their yips and calls reached my ears. A moment later I could hear the pop of their sticks and flushing whips.

"Over and behind only now, sir," Brian commanded, warning me that shooting out front could endanger the beaters.

Then the flagger on the right end of the line turned a single bird toward us. I took him high overhead with the first barrel.

"Take the full gun, sir," Brian said, jerking the half empty one from me and handing me its mate. "Behind only now!" he commanded.

One last bird raced by on my left. I let it get well behind me before pulling the trigger. Missing with the first barrel, I tried again and folded it with the second. Without that second shot I wouldn't have bagged it. The old boy was right again.

A horn sounded down the line. The drive was over.

"That's seven down," Brian said enthusiastically.

The beaters moved in around the butts, unsnapped the dogs from their leads, and allowed them to nose through the cover for downed birds.

"We had the best of it this morning. I suspect you're high gun, sir," Brian beamed.

Ah, what a beautiful phrase, "high gun." No poet ever penned a line so beautiful. It falls on the shotgunner's ear like cool water on parched lips. Suddenly one breathes deeply. One's chest swells. Life is good.

Actually seven grouse is not a big number. Lord Ripon would have probably thought it rather paltry. But these days it's respectable. And on this drive, I had shot more birds than anyone else. Needless to say, it went to my head. Things like that don't happen to me often. But I deserved it. I had taken hours of lessons and broken countless targets. And it had all paid off. On this trip to northern England, I had held my own with some very good wing shots.

Six months ago when I arranged to go on my first driven shoot, I knew about as much about it as I know about rocket science. Not much. I had hunted red grouse and ptarmigan over dogs in the Scottish Highlands. But hunting over dogs in Britain is much like hunting over dogs in America, and neither of those experiences replicates driven shooting. This time I would participate in that grand ritual involving beaters, loaders, and the exchange of guns. I was a little uneasy.

It didn't take long to encounter my first obstacle. I needed a "pair," a "brace," that is, two shotguns just alike. I went to see my old friend John Allen at Game Fair Ltd.

"John, I'm going on a driven shoot. I think I need a pair," I said confidently.

He smiled warmly in a way I hadn't seen before.

"Wonderful, wonderful, and I've got just the thing," he replied smoothly.

I was ushered into the gunroom where he unlocked one of the heavy steel drawers. I had never looked at a gun inside one of the locked drawers before. He pulled it out, opened the top on a dark leather case, and revealed a matched pair of Boss sidelocks.

"Wow," I whispered. "How much?"

"Fifty thousand," he answered.

What followed was a long silence during which John watched the color drain from my face. After a considerable length of time, he spoke, "Yes, they are a little pricey. Perhaps something else."

Unlocking another drawer, he showed me a pair of Westley Richards at thirty thousand. My face did not regain its color, and an uncontrollable twitch began in my left cheek.

"All right then, perhaps these?" he said, desperately pulling a pair of Spanish guns off the rack. "They're only fifteen thousand."

The twitch in my cheek slacked off a little, but not much.

"Okay," he said. "Let's get down to brass tacks. This is your first driven shoot, right?"

"Right," I answered.

"At this point you don't even know if you're going to like it, right?"

"That's true," I said.

"You may never shoot these guns again. So you don't want to spend that kind of money. Correct?"

"Yes," I said thankfully.

"All right, this is what I often recommend to people. Let's order two inexpensive shotguns for you in the same model. They won't be a true pair, but they'll be the same design with the same dimensions, and they'll look exactly alike. We can fix you up for about $2500. Which would you prefer, side-by-sides or over/unders?"

"But don't you have to shoot side-by-sides over there?" I asked.

"Not at all," he said. "What are you most comfortable with?"

"Well, I have been shooting over/unders a lot the last few years."

"Then over/unders it is," he said.

Now I began to realize the mess I'd gotten myself into. On the one hand, I didn't want to spend a fortune, but on the other hand ... suddenly I could see myself standing in the posh drawing room of an English manor house. Industrialist J. Finley Blight is sipping a glass of port and demonstrating the mount of one of his be-spoke Holland and Hollands. Lord Percy Pushbottom compliments him on his choice of fowling pieces. Lord Percy then puts down his Cubano Supremo, snaps the latch on a hand-tooled leather gun case, and brings forth one of his own matched pair of Woodwards, engraved with the Pushbottom family crest.

"Lovely, just lovely," J. Finley says admiringly.

Suddenly they turn to me. All my worst fears are realized. My nightmare is real.

"And what are you shooting, old boy?" they ask.

On the table in front of us is my cheap airline gun case. Inside it are two embarrassingly plain-looking little mass-produced O/Us. I'm about to be humiliated. What can I possibly do?

"But John, won't I be ... embarrassed?" I asked.

"Oh, there you go. You're a typical American, afraid you'll be embarrassed in front of the Brits. Well, if anyone asks, just tell them they're your travel guns."

"Travel guns?"

"Yes, as if you've got a pair at home so fine you never take them out of the safe."

"Oh."

"And after all, it's not like you're fibbing. You'll be traveling with these guns, won't you? That will make them your travel guns, right?"

"Right."

Now I really felt foolish. Why should I care what a bunch of Englishmen think? Am I a man or a wimp? I refuse to be judged by my possessions!

Travel guns, hmmm.

We ordered the two guns. John recommended the twenty-eight-inch barrels to help my swing and straight English stocks since that's what I'm used to. When they arrived, all that was needed was to add a 3/4-inch pad to each to increase the length of pull and accommodate my lanky frame. After the pads were added, the two little guns felt surprisingly good. They came to my shoulder perfectly and the sight plane fell right into place. I bought an ugly plastic airline case much like the one in my nightmare.

"The next thing you need to do is get busy practicing with them," John said. "You've got a lot of work to do."

I couldn't remember him ever seeing me shoot. But from the sound of that last comment, I had to assume that he had. He gave me the name of a local instructor who taught at a posh facility outside of town.

I finally found the place at the end of a long gravel road. As soon as I parked in front of the big redwood lodge, my new teacher bounded out the front door.

"I'm Roger Graham," he said in a pronounced cockney accent. "I understand you're up for a bit of instruction."

"Well, I'm going on my first driven shoot in a few months," I said, shaking his hand. "And to be honest, I don't want to make an ass of myself."

"I understand." He said, his manner suddenly becoming serious. Then he looked me over as if sizing me up.

"Let's try a few incoming, Governor," he suggested.

I took one of the O/Us out of its case and started to uncase the other.

"We'll only need one today, Captain," he said.

He didn't seem to notice the little gun's lack of elegance.

We walked down a hill and took our places on one of the shooting platforms. I did well on the first half dozen targets and was feeling pretty good about myself. Then he twisted a knob on his handheld remote. The next target almost took my hat off. As I began missing, he began fussing with my grip. Among other things, he moved my left hand in closer to my right.

"You're whipping the barrel a bit, Colonel," he said.

Then he started puttering with my feet. He placed them closer together so that I could turn more easily to my left and right. Then I learned to do a little pirouette and swing 180 degrees to the rear. Two weeks and several lessons later, I could see some improvement. But he kept pushing.

"Holy Sandringham! You don't expect me to hit these, do you?" I finally said in frustration.

The clays were so fast now I could hardly see them. By the time my brain registered that the target had been released, it had already passed me.

"You'll take a few out front, but this is where you'll kill most of your grouse, low and close in," he assured me. "And with a wind behind them, they'll be this fast or faster."

"Lord help me," I whispered.

Perspiration dripped down my neck, and a whole new twitch had developed in my right eye. I felt like an old machine being pushed to the limit. Like the *African Queen* when Humphrey Bogart kept feeding the old engine more and more coal and making it go faster and faster until it was close to flying to pieces.

"Pocata, pocata, pocata," went my pulse rate.

"That's all for today, Senator," he said, finally having mercy on me. "Next week, we'll start to work on pheasant shooting."

When next week came, we began with high overheads. Some were at the limits of my gun's range. And there were high lefts and rights where I learned to slump my right shoulder into the left-hand shots insuring that the barrel would move in a straight line.

In the meantime, I ordered a few clothes. I already owned two pairs of wool breeks or what we Americans sometimes mistakenly call "knickers." I also had knee socks, garters, and waterproof hiking shoes. For rough shooting in the Scottish Highlands I had only needed to add a waxed canvas coat and cap. But this was driven shooting, by golly, and I wanted to look the part. I ordered a tweed shooting jacket, a tattersall shirt, a wool cap, and a bright red tie with grouse flying across it.

Finally I was taught to shoot with a loader. At first we practiced with both guns empty. Later I understood why. As the two of us stood more or less facing in the same direction, I passed one gun to Roger with my right hand while taking the other from him with my left. In the beginning, it felt pretty clumsy. I even dropped one of the guns during an exchange. But as the lessons continued, my movements became smoother. Soon we were changing guns while actually shooting targets.

"There's one thing more," he said one afternoon. "There's something I can't teach you."

"What's that?" I asked.

"I can't teach you how to take grouse out front, the ones that are coming at you. It's very difficult to judge the distance. And you've got to remember their speed. So, just listen to your loader. He'll know."

Finally, toward the end of my last lesson, he suddenly said, "You're ready."

"I'm what?" I asked incredulously, afraid to be let go.

"You're ready, Major," he said. "You're as ready as I can make you."

Lord help me, I thought.

BOB WHITE

It is now several weeks later, and I'm in northern England. My four days of driven shooting are almost at an end. In the past three days, I've participated in five grouse and six pheasant drives, and I'm beginning to feel like a veteran.

There are eight guns on this trip, five Americans and three Englishmen. My companions are good sports and fine wing shots, and I find myself liking all of them. The landowner is called "Squire" or simply Charles. It seems there's some unresolved dispute about his rightful title. No matter, he and his wife have been wonderful hosts.

And as far as shooting goes, I've held my own. In fact I've developed a modest reputation. Last night at dinner, one of the pretty young wives, who had turned out to watch the afternoon pheasant drive, even paid me a compliment.

"Wow, you were great!" she said. "Every time you shot, a bird fell."

My gosh, she's talking to me, I thought, *and right here in front of the Squire and his wife and the flower of shotgun society.*

"Oh, bless you, my child," I wanted to say. "You don't know how much this moment means to me." Instead I said something appropriately humble.

It turns out that fine guns are not an issue here. No one ever sees a shooter's guns except him and his loader. They're put in cloth sleeves when they're taken to and from the gunroom to the field. Once a shooter takes his peg, that is his place in the line, his neighbors are too far away to see his guns. So no one ever saw mine. Not that it matters. I've made peace with my little pair of cookie-cutter shotguns. If I ever own a fine pair, it will be for the right reasons.

And I've learned something about clothes. Most of the veteran shooters now "dress down." In other words, they wear an old sweater and a tattered Barbour jacket above their breeks. It's the loaders and gamekeepers who dress up these days. They are decked out in neckties and the official estate tweeds.

I questioned an Englishman in our party who seemed to know his way around.

"Oh, yes, that's how it's done now," he said. "I guess you'd call it reverse snobbery."

But on the first day of nice weather, I couldn't help myself. I put on my tweed shooting jacket, my wool cap, my tattersall shirt, and my bright red tie with the grouse flying across it. I paid for it and, by golly, I was going to wear it. When we assembled on the front lawn to be assigned our pegs, my English friend looked me over questioningly.

"Reverse, reverse snobbery," I said.

He smiled back at me approvingly.

And now a horn sounds across the moor, signaling the beginning of the last grouse drive. Brian and I crouch a little lower in our butt. The beaters are still far below the crest of the hill and not visible. But a few scattered birds start to race in toward the center of the line. I hear shotguns popping in the distance. Brian hands me one of my two loaded guns. I bring it up close to my shoulder and feel a surge of adrenaline. Then three dots appear on the horizon in front of us. They are close to the ground, following the terrain, darting, veering. In the breadth of an instant, they are larger. And now I can just make out their silhouettes, the short powerful wings, the round torpedo-like bodies.

"Now, sir!" Brian shouts.

28

Swinton 98

From *Shooting Sportsman*

"He's claiming your birds, sir."

"Who?"

"In the next butt."

"You mean Fuzzman?"

"Well, no. Not Mr. Fuzzman, his loader."

I looked over at the next butt. Fuzzman's face was just visible above the little rock fence that marked the front edge of his bunker. He grinned and waved. His loader gazed into the distance like a retriever who'd just soiled the rug. In the excitement of the shoot, I hadn't noticed anything on either side of me. But Nigel, *my* loader, never missed anything.

"Nigel, why is he ...?"

"I suppose he's trying to save the gentleman some embarrassment. Mr. Fuzzman hasn't hit a bird all afternoon."

"Do you think he knows he hasn't hit a bird all afternoon?"

"I couldn't say, sir."

"But they haven't picked them up yet. How can he ...?"

"Mr. Fuzzman's loader has picked up two of yours."

"Oh."

This put me in an awkward position. I liked Fuzzman. He was an agreeable man. His opinions about things always seemed to be exactly the same as my own. Furthermore, if he was having a bad day, I was sympathetic. That could've been me over there. Sometimes, if I get off to a bad start, self-doubt creeps into my head. Then I get so I can't hit a bull in the behind with a boat paddle.

"Why can't we both claim them?" I asked.

"Then there'd be two birds unaccounted for. The gamekeeper wouldn't like that."

It was a day for bad starts. It was a freezing afternoon on the Earl of Swinton's estate in northern England with a wind strong enough to take your hat off. It's said that a red grouse can approach 100 mph with that kind of wind behind it. But in spite of everything, I was on my game. I'm not a great wing shot, it's just that shooting driven grouse agrees with me. There *is* no time for self-doubt, just enough to swing like hell and pull the trigger. It's a Zen thing.

"Forget it, Nigel. If we say something, we're going to look like a couple of girlie men."

"Sir?"

"You know, crybabies, tattletales. We should just let it go."

"That's probably best, sir."

We watched a group of birds race toward the far end of our line of butts. A half dozen shots reached our ears a second after three grouse tumbled into the heather out front. The remaining three sped on past, hugging the terrain like, well ... grouse.

"Nigel?"

"Sir?"

"If I hadn't hit a bird all afternoon, would you steal a couple from the next butt to save *me* from being embarrassed?"

"The situation hasn't come up, sir."

We had arrived at Swinton shortly before noon, and the earl himself met us at the carriage house. It was 1998, back when the old earl was still very much alive, and Swinton had not yet yielded to the demands of estate taxes and the lure of tourism.

"Ho, ho! Absolutely!" the earl shouted as each of us was introduced.

He was a huge man. I suspect his bloodline had benefited from a thousand years of good nutrition. The great manor house, the seat of his family for centuries, loomed behind him like some BBC movie set. After we'd all become acquainted, the earl's gamekeeper led us into the carriage house where a generous lunch was laid out. Several ladies from the house staff waited on us like doting aunts. The earl sat at the head of the table, extending far beyond the edges of his chair, and laughed uproariously at everything.

"Ho, ho, ho! Absolutely!" he bellowed.

After lunch we filed back outdoors. In an hour's time, the sky had grown dark, and the wind had picked up. The temperature was dropping like a shot put. The earl looked toward the high hills.

"I say, chaps. I should be paying *you* to go up there this afternoon, rather than you paying me. Ho, ho, ho absolutely!"

We said our good-byes and started the drive up to the moors. As we climbed, the road narrowed and the well-kept stonewalls along the sides gave way to low columns of rubble and ultimately to nothing. It seemed there was little on the high moors worth keeping in or out. Finally we arrived at a barren hilltop. When I stepped out of the vehicle, the wind cut through my clothes like a new pocketknife. I buttoned my coat up to the neck and pulled on the only gloves I had, a pair of paper-thin cape skin shooters.

"Dodgy weather," Nigel announced.

We started for the butts in single file, loaders and shooters, up and down hills, and in and out of gullies. Nigel insisted on carrying my little pair of O/Us. It was part of the job description. But I didn't protest. As an American, I had enough peripheral gear to justify hiring a pony. I hadn't noticed at the time, but our eighth gun, Mr. O'Neal, had not hiked out with us. He was a man in his late seventies, an Atlanta lawyer, who walked with difficulty and used a cane. Then I looked up and saw, of all things, what appeared to be a dune buggy bouncing across the moor. If it wasn't a dune buggy, it was a close relative, with wide balloon tires and a little rear engine. Sitting in the passenger seat, proud and erect as a peafowl, was Mr. O'Neal.

"Hey, Mr. O," Fuzzman called out from the next butt. "It looks like you decided to go in style!"

Mr. O'Neal acknowledged Fuzzman and me by tipping his hat. I waved cordially. *Hmmmm,* I thought. *This could add ten years to the effective life of a grouse shooter.*

In the beginning, our end of the line got the most shooting. I took two grouse out front and then one over my left shoulder. After several misses, I bagged two more behind our butt going away. Both times I had missed overhead shots with the first barrel. My flow state, or oneness with shotgun and target, was flagging. The gun on my right, a young fellow from California, was no slouch, and by that time, had probably downed the same number of birds I had or perhaps one more. Then, for a while, the action moved to the other end of the line. The wind began whistling off the muzzles of my shotgun like someone blowing on a jug.

"Warm enough, sir?" Nigel asked.

"I'll survive. You?"

"Oh, I'm fine," he lied.

I could feel the cold creeping in through my thin clothes. I was wearing a waxed canvas coat, a sweater, moleskin breeks, a cotton shirt, and a pair of wellies. Totally inadequate. The cold was an old familiar misery that reminded me of all the mornings I'd spent freezing my Texas keister off duck hunting back in the States. The coldest I remember being was one fifteen-degree morning when I waded out to retrieve a duck and stepped off up to my chest in a drainage ditch. Fortunately, I was only a couple of hundred yards from the lodge. I set off at a fast walk, not even bothering to look back.

"Are you ready, sir?" Nigel asked.

"What?"

"The beaters are getting closer," he said. "It'll be quite fast now for a few minutes."

"Oh, yes, I'm ready."

I brought one of my pair a little higher into my shoulder and squinted at the horizon like a serpent. A minute later, I could hear the beaters, too, their faint yips and hoots beyond the rise. Birds began diving off the crest of the hill like buzz bombs. They came in clutches of three to a half dozen before the stiff wind, hugging the landscape, going like wind-powered rockets. When they reached our line, the fire opened up. Grouse began falling in front of and around the butts like ripe fruit. Loaders shouted, coaxed, and cajoled, urging their shooters on.

"Now, sir!"

"And again, sir!"

"Your bird, sir!"

"Quickly, sir!"

The shots rolled and rippled up and down the line like artillery.

"This brace is yours, sir!" Nigel said suddenly. Two grouse had topped the rise like mortars lobbed from a bunker and were coming straight toward us.

"Now, sir!" Nigel said.

"Yes, but they're too far ..."

"Now, now, now!" Nigel shouted in my ear.

By the time I got the gun cheeked, the first grouse had traveled half the distance to our butt. I fired straight on and saw him cartwheel.

"And again!" Nigel commanded. He had dropped all semblance of decorum and was yelling at me like my fourth grade viola teacher. The second grouse swooped overhead, a mere blur. I pushed the barrels as hard as I could ahead of him and pulled the trigger. Too late.

"In front!" my loader shouted as he put the loaded shotgun into my left hand.

I dutifully shoved the empty one into his waiting grasp without taking my eyes off my targets. There were four of them, enough to cause a second of indecision, enough to insure failure when shooting at something as quick as a red grouse. Still, I managed to get my wits together in time to take the last of the group with my second barrel. Nigel and I exchanged guns again. A single bird sped toward us. I mounted the shotgun.

"Not your bird, sir!" he said as the grouse veered left.

It banked in over the top of Fuzzman's pit. I watched as he shouldered his shotgun and swung overhead. But he had underestimated the bird's speed. The arc of his swing was too near its end, too far spent. He took an awkward step backward, firing twice. The grouse flew on untouched. Then the beaters topped the rise in front of us.

"No more shooting, sir," Nigel said.

The drive was over. The beaters and pickers-up moved in among the butts with their dogs, sleek black Labs anxious for work. They were of all stripes: teenagers, young girls, middle-aged women, and older men. They were farm workers, villagers, and local gentry, happy for a chance to use their dogs and participate in an afternoon of sport, even if only in a supporting role. This game shooting was a spectacle that squeamish Londoners wanted to outlaw, people whose only knowledge of the outdoors came from Hyde Park and the telly. With a ban on fox hunting pending, country people knew that shooting was also in the crosshairs.

"I don't suppose you'll be high gun now," Nigel said, intruding on my thoughts.

"High gun? Well, no I never expected ..."

"With that brace of birds that Mr. Fuzzman claimed, I suspect you'd have been on top."

"No kidding?"

"Yes, sir."

"Nigel, are you telling me you know how many grouse everyone else on the line has bagged?"

"Yes, more or less."

I didn't doubt Nigel. He'd probably seen more grouse drives than Lord Walsingham. Loaders are a mysterious bunch anyway and with dark powers. One does not question.

"What about Fuzzman? Did he ever ...?"

"I don't think so."

"And you're saying I might be high gun, that is, counting those two grouse that Fuzzman's loader ... uh, stole?"

"Counting those two, yes."

"Then perhaps we should reconsider ..."

I stared away at the rolling hills, the ankle-deep vegetation stretching into the distance. Tonight there would be dinner with the wives and sweethearts back at Constable Burton. Much of the talk would be about the afternoon's shoot. I could see myself being congratulated, slapped on the back, and jokingly called Bogardus or Lord Ripon, and me basking in my glory, pretending modesty, mumbling about good luck and drawing the best butt. On the other hand, if I claimed that brace of grouse, it would leave Fuzzman with a bird count for the afternoon of zero. Furthermore, telling on him and his loader, whether he knew about the theft or not, would humiliate him.

Okay, Fuzzman, take those two birds with my best wishes. I've been there. I've seen days when I couldn't hit the floor with a watermelon. If I can save your pride, I'm happy to do it. One day I may need a similar favor from some other benevolent soul. So I'm putting one in the bank. Karma. I'm not concerned about Nigel because I know he won't say a word. Embarrassing one of the paying guns would be out of the question. So it's up to me, and I promise to keep my mouth shut for ten years. But then all bets are off.

29

Ten Rules for Shooting with Englishmen

By Floyd C. Hoggenback

From *Shooting Sportsman*

I'll bet you've dreamed about shooting across the "big pond" all your life. You know what I mean, England! Yeah! Lord Ripon, matched pairs, "Jolly well done" and all that! Well, me too. As a matter of fact, I'd dreamed about it and talked about it for years.

When I first started, Wanda was pretty nice about what she called my "England thing." For a while she even seemed to be interested in it. But later on when I brought it up, she'd get that look on her face, the same one she used to get when I'd bring out my Slim Whitman records. Then she'd stare at her fingernails. I don't know what it was that was so blamed interesting about her fingernails. But she kept looking at them ... and the ceiling.

Anyway, things went on like that for a long time, you know, me dreaming about shooting in England and reading about it. But I never thought I'd actually get the chance to go. Then something happened that made me want to go even more. I sort of accidentally put together my own pair of shotguns. You see when you shoot in England, you need two shotguns just alike. You have a fellow called a *loader* who loads one while you shoot the other. But I'll bet you already knew that. Okay, what I put together was not a real pair but what they call a "composed pair." I already had a 12 gauge over/under that I'd won in a bingo game at the Moose Lodge. I found another one just like it secondhand at a gun show. Then I got a snappy-looking cap like the ones I'd seen in *The Field*. The best thing of all was when I discovered a tweed suit at the consignment store, the kind with those short pants they wear over there. To top it all off, I ordered a red silk tie with pheasants on it out of a catalog.

Well ... I suppose I talked about England so much that Wanda finally saw what it would mean to me to actually go. So one evening when I was sitting there in my outfit describing the great estates, the high pheasants, the kale fields and all, she came right out with it. I guess she'd been saving it up for a surprise.

"Go to England, damn you!" she yelled.

"What, Wanda?"

"You heard me! Go! I can't take it anymore!"

"But, Wanda, it's so expensive and ..."

"Take your son's college fund! Blow it. I don't care!"

I thought that was quite understanding of her. And I decided right then to take her up on the offer. Anyway, does the world *really* need another brain surgeon? So I booked my trip. Later on the fellow at the gun store told me I'd hit the jackpot. He said my shoot was the "real deal," and I was darned lucky to get it.

So ... the trip went great. Well, almost. Okay, there were a few little snags. You see there were one or two things I didn't know about. No big deal, just something they call *appropriate behavior*. But never mind that. The good news is, you're in luck. Because I took everything I learned over there and made up ten rules. So if you ever get a chance to go across the "big water," you'll know exactly what to do

Here are Floyd C. Hoggenback's ten rules for shooting with Englishmen:

Rule 1: I'll bet you already know this one. Don't call them knickers. It turns out those short pants they wear for shooting are called *plus-fours* or *breeks*. In England knickers are underwear. Now that you know that, you won't be one of those dumb Americans who says, "In my country, we don't wear knickers." If you do happen to say that and they all laugh and tell you that knickers are underwear, you can always pretend that you knew it all along and you really *were* talking about underwear.

Rule 2: On some estates they have white pheasants. That's right, snow-white pheasants. They're special birds bred for their white feathers. I was told they're put with the ordinary pheasants so the gamekeeper can find a flock in thick cover. Everyone will warn you not to accidentally shoot a white pheasant. And whatever you do, don't. If you do, it's not only considered *bad form*, you'll also have to pay a big fine. You could be in quite a mess if you don't have enough cash on hand. Thank heaven they'll accept a check.

Rule 3: When your loader speaks to another person about "the gentleman," don't look around for somebody hiding in the trees. Your loader is talking about *you*. He might say something like, "the gentleman shot five brace," which would mean you shot ten pheasants since over there a "brace" means two. On the other hand, you might overhear him saying something like, for example, "the gentleman couldn't hit the bloody floor with a pudding."

Another thing about loaders is they are really, really fussy. When your loader thinks that a bird is closer to the guy on your left or the guy on your right than to you, he'll say, "Not your bird, sir." When he thinks the bird is too low and it's not a sporting shot, he'll say, "Too low, sir." When he thinks the bird is too high and you might only "prick" it, he'll say, "Too high, sir." By the time he says, "Your bird, sir," you're likely to be two thirds of the way through a Snickers Bar. Furthermore, if you get lucky and actually shoot a grouse or a pheasant, you're supposed to stand there as still as a fern and not say a word. Under no circumstances (this is important) do you holler out, "Shazam!" or "I'm smoking, baby!"

Rule 4: Don't wear striped ties. As sure as you wear one, it will turn out to be the official tie of the 32nd Royal Kent Fusiliers or some such thing. And someone who was in the 32nd Royal Kent Fusiliers will be sitting across from you at dinner. He'll know you weren't in the darned thing because he doesn't remember you. And he'll expect you to be embarrassed about wearing his precious regiment's tie. And you'll say, "Look, I thought it was just a tie." Anyway, I don't even know what a fusilier is. You might also avoid those ties with little crests on them. I believe those are mostly taken too. It turns out that ties with pheasants are okay. More on that later. Or you could get one with dots. I don't think they care about dots. And here's the kicker. I found out Englishmen don't just have special ties for regiments. They have them for clubs and schools and towns and who knows what all? There's a joke they tell over there that goes: When three Americans get together, they start a business. When three Frenchmen get together, they start a restaurant. When three Englishman get together, they start a club. And as sure as Lady Di was a babe, when those three Englishmen start their club, they're going to want their own tie.

Rule 5: Don't expect great food. If you're shooting, you'll be staying at a house, a lodge, an inn, or something. In other words, you'll be out in the country. That's where the real English people live. Don't think the great dinner you had when you stayed overnight in London was English food. A Frenchman probably cooked it. Out in the country, you'll get lots of roast beef. And when they say roast beef, that's what they mean. They roast it and roast it and roast it. At dinner, there might be a big assortment of silverware around your plate. You probably won't know what to do with most of it. But I can save you some time and trouble. None of it has much effect on the roast beef.

And speaking of food, if you're lucky enough to shoot a bird, don't think they're going to let you take it home with you. I mean even if you could take it all the way back to the States, they wouldn't give it to you. It turns out pheasant and grouse are worth big money. So they sell them to expensive restaurants in London where Frenchmen cook them. As far as a pheasant dinner one night during your shoot, forget about it. You'll be having roast beef.

Rule 6: Don't dress up for shooting. I won't mention any names, but certain Americans have been known to go prancing out on the first day dressed up in a tweed suit, shooting cap, and red silk tie with pheasants on it. Well, it turns out that's not the *proper thing* anymore. If you've read about the days when Lord Walsingham and Lord Ripon and all those people were around, and the shooters looked like lords ... forget it. These days the shooters wear old short pants, I mean breeks, and mangy sweaters. The ideal shooting outfit would be a really, really old pair of short pants and a really, really old sweater. But of course you don't have any really, really old English shooting clothes because it's your first freakin' trip to shoot in England for heaven's sake! I guess the next best thing would be to take your spiffy outfit and leave it in the middle of the interstate for a few days. For rainy weather, you'll need a waterproof hunting coat. If your old one finally got so ragged you gave it to the kid who mows your lawn, try to get it back. You should bring a necktie with you. But it's not to wear when you're shooting. You're supposed to wear it at dinner. Like I said, one with pheasants on it is okay. But just to be safe, I'd go with the dots.

Rule 7: You won't believe this. It's the loaders who dress up in tweed suits and neckties for shooting these days. So the loaders look like they should be shooters, and the shooters look like they should be loaders. If I hadn't told you about that, you'd have probably done something dumb like telling some lord to run back to the house and get your camera. And then everyone would expect you to be really embarrassed and apologize and everything. And you'd be thinking, *How was I supposed to know he was a lord? He looked like he'd just crawled out of a Dumpster!*

Rule 8: Don't pick up anything. Don't even *offer* to pick up or carry anything. The English have something called the *class system*. I found out the loaders (the ones who are all dressed up) carry all the gear and do all the work. The shooters (the ones who are dressed like bums) do nothing but shoot. You might see your loader huffing and puffing along behind you with your shotguns, your shell bag, thermos bottle, camera, and all your other stuff. The American way would be to pitch in, do your part, and share the load. But no. That's not the English way. You're supposed to strut along in front of the man like a debutante who's just put on nail polish. But I think it's all part of the act anyway. The more work your loader acts like he's doing, the bigger tip he expects.

And speaking of picking up things, it turns out you're not even supposed to pick up your own birds! There are people called *pickers-up* who come in with their dogs when the shoot's over and find all the birds. You're very lucky I told you about this. You could have been like that ignorant American I heard about who yelled out, "Excuse me, lady, that happens to be my pheasant you've got there!"

Rule 9: You'll notice that Englishmen like telling jokes about Frenchmen, Germans, Italians, Scots, Australians, and anybody else they can think of. A lot of Americans think that kind of thing is in bad taste. So, if you feel that way, I guess you could just ignore it or leave the room. But if it doesn't bother you, you can always join in and laugh right along with them. After all, what could be more fun than getting in there and guffawing with the natives, you know, being one of the boys? But one thing I should warn you about ... it turns out they don't like jokes about Englishmen.

Rule 10: There's something else I want to say about tipping. When you get your final bill, you'll see a big charge there for your loader's services. And after you pay the bill, they'll tell you that you should also give your loader a big tip. And you'll think, "Gosh, I've already paid the man a fortune." Then they'll tell you that you should tip the gamekeeper, the cook, the housemaids, and heaven knows whom else. You're expected to pass out all those tips the morning you leave. When you see how much it adds up to, you'll probably be tempted to pack your gear and slip down the back stairs while everyone else is still asleep. Ha, ha, ha. But if you decide to do that, make sure you look out for the butler. It turns out those fellows get up really early.

Anyway, there you have Floyd C. Hoggenback's ten rules for shooting with Englishmen. Learn them, and you'll sail through your first trip without a hitch. You'll know all about what they call the *proper thing*. You might think I'm being nitpicky with all this, but the truth is this stuff is pretty important. In fact, it seems that if you break one of the rules you could be, well ... disinvited. That's right. You might be told to never come back to Splay on Spivey on Thames or wherever it is again. But listen ... if that happens, don't worry. I know a place in Scotland that will take you.

30

Pigeons in Plaid

From *Shooting Sportsman*

"Comin' at you, cousin!" Reggie yelled.I stood up and swung the barrels hard past the blue-gray streak that rocketed past me. But at the last second, it seemed to sense my presence. It darted skyward as if catapulted from a slingshot. When I yanked the trigger, only blue sky was there. Then, incredibly, the bird swooped back down to its original trajectory like a World War II Spitfire.

"Damn!" I said out loud as I crouched back in the fencerow.

We were spread out about thirty yards apart, hidden in the thick bracken surrounding a Scottish bean field. Reggie Taylor, my new friend from South Carolina, was stationed at the corner. Juan, one of our guides, was to his left. I held down the third position to Reggie's right. On open ground, about thirty yards downwind, were a dozen carefully placed pigeon decoys.

We were in a far-flung corner of the Duke of Atholl's 300,000-acre estate in central Scotland. The holder of these lands isn't merely a duke. He is also head of the Murray Clan, that is, the Murrays of Atholl, not to be confused with the Murrays of Polmaise, Abercairney, or Auchtertyre. The chief of the Atholl Murrays resides at Blair Castle. There he is protected by his official bodyguard, the Atholl Highlanders. This little troop is the last official private army in the queen's realm.

Suddenly, four more gray specks came shooting up the center of the field like bottle rockets. They were headed directly at the corner. I knew Reggie saw them, but I couldn't help calling out.

"Reggie! Up the middle!" I shouted.

He and Juan (pronounced Joo-an) stood up at the same moment. But just as the shots sounded, the two lead birds darted sideways. One flew on unscathed. The other slowed and fluttered into the thicket behind them. The second pair veered and darted out of range.

It was Reggie's third miss in a row. A stream of epithets came pouring out of the briars where he stood that would have scalded the ears of a duck guide. He was calling these creatures everything from deviants to Bolsheviks. Funny what a little bird can do to a man, even a man as amiable as Reggie.

"Behind you, lad," Juan shouted at me, interrupting him.

I jumped to my feet as a single pigeon came streaking overhead. My barrels swung smoothly past its head, and I fired. But at the last second, my target cut to the left, leaving me, again, with only thin air.

"Can you believe that?" I yelled in frustration.

"Therrr seein' us lads. We got to stee doon," Juan called out.

Juan was from the Isle of Mann, a Manx. His Gaelic accent was even thicker than that of the local Scots.

Of course. That's it. They're seeing us, I said to myself. *All right, if I've got to 'stee doon' then I'll 'stee doon.' From now on my rear end is glued to the ground.* Reggie and Juan had assumed the same strategy. A group of five birds came sailing over the decoys toward their positions. This time when the pigeons reached the hedgerow, there was not a hint of movement, only the pop of two shotguns. My two partners were crouched low in the thick vegetation, invisible. The first two birds tumbled into the grass behind them, and the other three scattered.

"Okay, now that I know the drill," I said, talking out loud to the imaginary bird god, "Send me a pigeon!"

Who knows what had prompted Juan to take us on this wild pigeon shoot? But when he suggested it, only Reggie and I, out of the seven guns in our party, had agreed to go along. Everyone else had stayed back at the lodge nursing sore feet. And who could blame them? We had been shooting grouse over dogs in the Grampian Highlands for the last four days. And pursuing grouse over dogs requires a damnable amount of walking. After averaging five to seven miles a day up and down those craggy moors, we looked like the Scottish army returning from Dunbar.

But when Juan swept through the lodge, saying he had located a field where wood pigeons were feeding, for some reason, I picked up my shotgun and shell bag and limped after him. Reggie Taylor was the only other taker. When I reached the front door, he was already squeezing himself into the backseat of Juan's tiny car. Reggie had endless stamina and no sense of pain. I slid into the front seat.

BOB WHITE

"We can't shoot birds lying around in bed. Can we, cousin?" Reggie said, slapping me on the back.

The night our shooting party arrived, Reggie, my fellow southerner, and I had stayed up past the others for a final drink. He became convinced sometime during the course of the evening that we were related.

We set up in a four- or five-acre field beside a country lane. The beans had been harvested recently, and there was plenty of waste on the ground. Several hours of daylight remained, and Juan was sure the pigeons would be back. It turned out he was right.

"Look ta ya rright, lad!" he called out.

A pair of birds came barreling down my edge of the field as if they were carrying an urgent message. I sat still. At the last possible second, I lifted myself a little off my haunches and onto my knees. The front bead swung past the first bird, and I pulled the trigger. This time he was still there. He folded in a corona of feathers and fell about twenty yards out in the field. The second veered to the right, and I sent a squandered shot after it. But things were looking up. After making sure there were no more pigeons in the air, I trotted out to pick up my trophy. What I found surprised me. It was about sixteen inches long counting its tail feathers, twice the size of a mourning dove.

"Hey, look at this thing! It's as big as a mallard," I exaggerated.

"I know," Reggie called back in his Carolina accent. "It makes a man think they're right up close when they're really not."

Ah, now he's got something there, I thought. After a lifetime of shooting mourning doves, as Reggie and I had, shooting at a bird that looked much like it but is twice its size could throw off a man's judgment. I now had a lovely excuse for missing these things. I mentally filed it away in case I needed it.

Not only was the bird's size notable, but also its coloration. It was mostly gray, but there were distinctive white armbands and a snow-white collar. The sides of its neck were glossy purple and green. The most striking feature, however, was the bright yellow eyes. The wood pigeon is the only member of the pigeon family to have them.

It is one of Britain's ten most plentiful birds. Numbers are estimated at seven to ten million. In winter they form huge flocks, feeding in fields and pastures in the daytime and roosting in groves at night. According to tradition, its call is not a statement but a question.

It asks, "Who cooks for you, oh?" three to five times and then ends with a quick, "Who?"

They are voracious eaters. One shooter reportedly found a single bird's craw stuffed with 370 grains of corn. Multiply that by hundreds or even thousands, and you can understand the damage they exact. They also enjoy the nuts of beech trees, vegetable crops, and other grains. Needless to say, most farmers prefer their pigeons dead. It's relatively easy to get a landowner's permission to hunt these birds. For obvious reasons, the farmer wants any indigenous flocks either reduced or forced to move on.

Wood pigeon shooting in Britain is categorized as rough shooting. That means it is not formal, driven shooting or game shooting. But in fact, anything that is not game shooting is called rough shooting. It's true that it's a favorite of those who can't afford the expense of shooting pheasant or grouse. But it's also enjoyed by the more fortunate since it provides a great way of getting the old skills up to speed. The cost is minimal. Whereas a day of driven pheasant shooting in Britain might cost you $800, and a day of driven grouse $1000, pigeon shooting can be had, complete with guide, for as little as $150 a day.

Gunners who indulge in it, no matter what their circumstances, take it seriously. Pigeons are, for the most part, hunted over decoys. The truth is, that's the only way you're going to get close to one. A wood pigeon, unlike its central park cousin, is a truly wild bird. If you were to attempt to walk up on a flock, you probably wouldn't get closer than 150 yards. And as far as sneaking up on them behind a rock wall or fencerow, forget it. They rarely feed within 100 yards of any cover that might conceal a predator. The only way you're going get close enough for a shot is with trickery.

The whole thing is carried out much like a goose hunt. First locate a field where the pigeons are feeding. Next set out a dozen or so decoys about twenty-five yards downwind from where you hope to conceal yourself. Aficionados claim that the decoys must all be facing into the wind and should be no more than three feet apart. You may increase the size of your decoy spread as you shoot birds. Dead birds can be set up along with the deeks. But purists insist that they must have their heads propped up with sticks or clods of dirt. Otherwise the pigeons in the air will know something is amiss. This seems to me to be quite a testament to the wariness and keen eyesight of these critters.

Next you conceal yourself. If the field is large and open, a pigeon hunter builds a blind. This is done with bales of straw or with netting laced with grass or stubble. He may also cut some branches and sticks and hide himself in a fencerow. Serious pigeon shooters go to extreme measures to be invisible. They claim that wood pigeons have some of the sharpest eyes of any game bird. You won't be surprised to hear that they wear camouflaged clothing especially made to blend with the vegetation they're hiding in. But they also cover their faces with veils and wear gloves to conceal their hands. Some prefer smearing their faces and hands with dirt. Wrist watches, glasses, gun barrels, and anything else that might reflect light must be covered.

If the decoy spread is realistic enough and the shooter is well enough hidden, the birds may come in close enough for a shot. Wood pigeons fly fast and straight. But if a bird sees you, it can dodge and veer with amazing agility. So the trick is to keep yourself concealed until the last possible moment. Some shooters try to mount the gun, stand up, and fire in one quick movement. Others shoot on their knees or from a sitting position.

The record wood pigeon bag for a single day by one gun is 550 birds. Major

Archie Coats, a professional pigeon guide, accomplished this in January 1962. To an American, these numbers sound excessive. But things are different over there. Wild game is not the property of the public but of the landowner. And I assume the landowner was happy to be rid of what he considered a nuisance.

And I'm reasonably sure those birds were not wasted. Wood pigeons are very good eating and are therefore on the menus in many European restaurants. The meat is dark and nutty, much like a dove. But unlike a dove, a single bird is large enough to make up an entree. They are usually served rare and accompanied by a sauce based on wine or fruit. I'm confident that that thrifty English landowner got what was coming to him for them.

"Herrr they come, lads," Juan called out, making me involuntarily duck my head.

By then Reggie had downed a half dozen pigeons, and Juan wasn't far behind. With each lull in the shooting, one of them ran onto the field and set out his dead birds. Juan was careful to follow protocol, propping up each one's head with a stick or clod of dirt. Our decoy spread was getting larger but with little thanks to me.

Using my pocketknife, I'd built myself a suitable hiding place in the hedgerow. There was ample brush around me to put up reasonably dense walls in front and on both sides. I was invisible from three directions.

In late afternoon the birds began descending on us in groups of two to twenty. Swooping through the open field, they eyed the decoys and rocketed toward the perimeters, only to turn above the rock walls and hedges and sail back toward the middle for a second look. We were popping away. At times, Hundreds of pigeons were in the air. I began to get my range and drop birds consistently. Some went by like clay targets from a machine wound up too tight. Others fluttered over, changing directions and making easy targets of themselves.

"Behind you, Reggie!"

"Juan, on your right!"

"Comin' right at ya, lad!"

The numbers piled up, but there was to be no waste. We were on the Duke of Atholl's estate where every bird and bunny is carefully accounted for. Pigeons aren't worth as much as pheasant and certainly not grouse, but they still have value. That evening, Juan would turn them over to the head keeper. They would be counted, tagged, and hung overnight in a cool room. A game broker would pick them up in the morning. I may have eaten one of those very pigeons the next week in London.

"Heads up, cousin!" Reggie yelled.

A half dozen birds came speeding down my edge of the field in the fading light. Without thinking, I swung past the first one and pulled the trigger. I saw it go limp. The others veered wildly, but I followed the one closest in. The barrels passed in front of it, and I wasn't even conscious of pulling the trigger. But the bird tumbled.

Two more followed in their wake. I had to reload quickly. It's a clumsy thing reloading a side-by-side while sitting on the ground in thick cover. There's no room, no freedom of movement. I pushed open the action, and the muzzles hit the ground in front of me. Now there was dirt in the ends of the barrels. The two shells in my right hand fell into the grass. In the confusion I forgot myself and stood up.

"'They're comin' in, lad! Git doon!" Juan shouted.

31

Miles and Miles of Heather

From *Shooting Sportsman*

"Watch your spaniel, gentlemen. Watch your spaniel," Ben called out.

The little black and white dog had slowed her pace. She was wagging her tail excitedly and tiptoeing forward. Finally, she eased her hind end down into a sitting position, her eyes fixed on a spot in the heather in front of her.

"Kack kack," came the warning call.

Then a dozen grouse burst into the air, their wings thundering. They exploded outward, like a simulation of the "big bang," each reaching for space.

"Mark," Ben shouted.

Two shotguns sounded. One grouse tumbled into the heather, and another fluttered off to the right.

"And again!" the gamekeeper commanded.

Two more reports came from the gunners nearest the covey, but the remaining birds had put some distance behind themselves by then. They rocketed across the heather untouched.

"Reload quickly," Ben shouted.

Proving him right, a final grouse took to the air. Both shooters fired, and it dropped in a mist of feathers.

"Hold your line please, gentlemen," Ben called out.

The birds had not flushed in front of me. I stood obediently where I was, watching the action some fifty yards up the line.

The little spaniel nosed out the two dead birds and brought them to his master. The third, which had limped to the end of the line, came under the jurisdiction of John's yellow Labrador.

When all the grouse were collected, Ben looked up and down the eighty-yard line of men. Seeing everything to his satisfaction, he ordered us forward again.

"On we go slowly," he called out in his Scottish burr.

There were nine of us that day: Ben Furney, head gamekeeper, Kevin, his under keeper, John, and Juan (pronounced Joo-an), two more keepers who worked part-time on the estate, and five American shooters or "tenants." We were placed in line about thirty feet apart with guns and keepers alternating. Ben and the other three keepers did not shoot. Instead, each carried a long staff topped with polished stag horn. The dogs, one in front of each of them, were a collection of two Labs, one yellow and one black, and two spaniels.

This was not some thrown together afternoon of rough shooting. This was shooting over dogs or "dogging grouse" in the old tradition. In Scotland, where red grouse are more scattered and the terrain more rugged, it is often impossible to organize driven shoots. So in some areas, rough shooting has evolved into a rather formal ritual. To see a long line of men striding a moor in this way, with four or five dogs quartering ahead of them, is quite a spectacle.

Ben Furney ran our line like a regiment of Black Watch. Every move and every step were carefully choreographed. And I don't doubt that it was all necessary. Moving a file of men eighty to 100 yards long evenly across a mountainside is not easy. Without his leadership, the event would have degenerated into something resembling a fraternity house fire drill.

He looked like a lithograph from a turn-of-the-century issue of *The Field*. Tall and gray and as straight as a cudgel, he wore the official tweeds of the Duke of Atholl's estate and sported a handlebar mustache. Every morning there was a fresh sprig of heather in his lapel.

"A wee bitee to the rrright gentlemen," he bellowed out.

Dutifully, we edged the line toward the right, moving higher up the face of the moor. All we needed was a piper. We could've done battle with the English.

"Watch your black dog!" Ben suddenly shouted.

It was Juan's Lab that was birdie this time. These Labs didn't quite point. Instead they slowed, sniffed the air, and began to creep forward like house cats. The dog was immediately to my left. If grouse flushed, they'd be in my ballpark.

"Studeee, studeee," Juan called as the dog eased ahead.

"Kack kack kack kack," came the shrill alarm call.

Too quickly, they erupted in front of me. I wasn't ready.

"Mark!" Ben yelled.

Mounting my gun frantically, I foolishly shot into the middle of the rising whirlwind of grouse. Nothing fell. Reggie Taylor, a big, strapping fellow from South Carolina, was on Juan's other side. Out of the corner of my eye, I saw two birds go down. I knew that neither of them was mine. Thankfully, a latecomer rose a heartbeat behind the rest, and I was able to take him as he turned right.

"Reload quickly!" Ben commanded.

I clumsily put two fresh cartridges into my old Scott. But there were no more grouse.

Covey fever is not limited to Georgia, I thought.

There I was, 3 1/2 days into the trip, and I was still jumping through my hat every time birds flushed. I found that I was never quite mentally prepared at the moment when they came up in front of me. Grouse over dogs are supposedly easier to shoot than driven grouse. But you couldn't prove it by me. With driven grouse you don't have that damnable surprise factor. You can see the bloomin' thing coming.

By then the sun was straight overhead. We had arrived at a rock-strewn creek, and Ben decided it was a good place to have lunch. He called to our two pony boys, who'd been leading a little white pony behind our line all morning. They led the shaggy little beast up into our midst and began unloading the big baskets or "panniers" it carried on its back. The boys laid out beef sandwiches, oranges, and yogurt. Each of us was presented with a single warm beer.

After I had eaten, I stretched out in the heather and pulled my cap down over my face. I was tired, and my feet hurt. And I wasn't alone, at least among the Americans. It was our fourth day of shooting, and we had been making five to seven miles a day over pretty rough ground. These were the Grampians, the highest of the Scottish Highlands. They weren't the Andes, but they were rugged enough to exact some wear and tear. Perhaps I should've been in better shape.

Dick Hummel, one of the older men, plopped down beside me in the heather with a sigh.

"Look at that," he said, pointing toward Ben.

I looked over and saw that Ben was already on his feet. He was leaning on his staff, surveying the country ahead, anxious to get moving.

"He's not human," Dick said.

Soon we were tramping forward again, our football field-length line undulating across the moor like some giant serpent. The order had been reshuffled, and Kevin was immediately to my left. He looked like Ben in miniature. Dressed in the same suit of estate tweeds and moleskin cap, he was Ben's downsized duplicate. At seventeen, he would be under keeper for another fifteen or twenty years. When Ben was too old to walk the moors, Kevin would finally take his place. Jobs were scarce here in the Highlands.

"Git bok here, mon!" Ben called to his spaniel.

The dog was working too far ahead of us.

"Git bok here, I said!"

Just then, the little English Spaniel abruptly sat down in the heather and fixed his gaze on a spot in front of him.

"Easy, gentlemen," Ben said as we eased the line forward.

The dog was just to my right. I raised my gun a little higher and vowed this time I wouldn't succumb to panic. Up they came with a roar. There were eight or ten grouse, each intent on a different direction.

"Mark!" Ben shouted.

One bird flew almost straight away from me. As the gun reached my shoulder, I blotted out the escaping form and fired. It dropped like a stone. Another veered to the right, directly in front of my position. He was already at full speed when I pushed the barrels by him. As the front bead passed his head, I felt the recoil and knew I had pulled the trigger. The bird tumbled.

"Reload quickly!" Ben shouted.

Fumbling in my shell bag, I found two more cartridges. I slipped them into the waiting chambers and stood tensed and ready. But no more grouse came up.

"Well shot, sir," Ben called, sending his dog into the cover to pick up the two dead birds.

Say it louder, Ben, I thought. *Shout it from the rooftops. Let the word go forth to all nations. Three and a half days into this, hunt and I've finally shot a double.*

We passed a ruined croft that afternoon. All that remained were four tumbled-down walls, the remnants of a stone farmhouse standing incongruously in an ocean of heather. It was a reminder of the Highland Clearances of the early and mid-1800s. During that period, thousands of people left the region. Some simply grew tired of the poverty and stinginess of the soil. Others were forced off the land. Certain lords and chieftains, to whom these people had been loyal for centuries, began to prefer the profitability of sheep. Many of these dislocated Highland Scots went to America.

The five to seven miles a day were beginning to wear us down. Two of the older men were asking for more frequent rest stops. My feet were killing me, but I was too proud to let on. Still, I was thankful each time Ben called a halt.

We flushed two roe deer that afternoon. They sprang up out of the cover right at our feet. Tiny creatures, weighing only about thirty-five pounds, they bounded away, looking surprisingly delicate, as if they might be too fragile to survive here. Then we spotted a herd of red deer crossing a craggy peak in the distance. There were several big stags in the group with ornate antlers. They looked and moved like caribou or reindeer, nothing at all like the whitetail deer I was used to.

"How many birds do we have, Ben?" I asked.

"Ten breece," he said." It's na enough."

A brace being two, we had twenty birds. We finished the day with sixteen brace. Ben still wasn't satisfied.

The last day began with a hard climb. We started at the base of a rocky slope and followed the faint outline of a trail that went almost straight up. Scratching and clawing with one free hand, we held our shotguns clear with the other. When we reached the top, we were standing on a broad moor. It swept in a wide arc between the steep drop on our left and rocky outcroppings on our right.

A local Scot, Pat McCormick, who was even more elegantly dressed than our keepers, had joined us that morning. He took his place in line, showing great respect for Ben Furney. That gave us a total of ten men. We moved higher and higher most of the afternoon.

The four keepers urged their dogs on, bullying and coaxing.

"Haroo, haroo," John called.

"Loocy, Loocy," Kevin said, encouraging his Lucy.

"Git bok here, mon!" Ben scolded.

"Studee, studee," Juan purred.

This is one of the last settings in Britain where setters are used as they were originally intended. Once all British bird shooting was done over dogs. But things changed. With the advent of the breech-loading shotgun in the mid-1800s, it became much easier to shoot big numbers of birds. When Edward VII bought Sandringham expressly to pursue his interest in driven shooting, the writing was on the wall.

That afternoon we were high enough to flush ptarmigan. They took to the air about fifty yards ahead of our line, too far out for a shot. We watched them sail over the next peak, dazzlingly white in the sunlight.

When we reached the top of the last craggy pinnacle, it seemed as if we were on top of the world. There were no fence, no village, no tree, nothing to break up the continuity of landscape, only endless heather and sky, purple and blue. In a glen far to the north, I saw the azure blue glitter of a hidden loch.

Suddenly grouse were everywhere! Every twenty or thirty yards, one of the dogs stiffened and nosed the air.

"Watch your spaniel!" Ben yelled.

Or it might be the "black dog" or "yellow dog."

"Mark!"

"Kack kack kack," went the call as each flock took to the air, wings ablur.

"And again!" Ben shouted.

"Well shot."

"Reload quickly!"

"Well shot."

"And again!" he called.

We were scrambling over rocks, trying to stay in line and watch the dogs at the same time.

"Straighten your line please, gentlemen!" he shouted.

"Come forward please, Mr. Hummel."

I found my rhythm. I began to shoot better than I really can, the way I sometimes do when I don't have time to think. The aching in my feet disappeared. I was no longer tired. My senses became more acute and my reactions quicker. Our line moved through the heather and rocks methodically, with singleness of purpose. The number of bagged birds mounted.

Then I fell headlong into a gully. I'd been watching the dog on my left and suddenly felt myself step out into nothingness. Thankfully, I fell onto soft peat. But my adrenaline was flowing. Without thinking, I scrambled up the other side, cutting my hand on an exposed root. Later, Reggie Taylor would show me the black and blue shins he'd accumulated that afternoon.

And then it was over. For about twenty minutes, the shooting had been frantic. But it ended as abruptly as it had started. We had shot thirty-two brace, sixty-four birds. All that was left was the long walk down the mountain as we nursed bruises and sore feet.

But it was not to be a leisurely stroll.

"Form your line, please, gentlemen," Ben called out.

We were to take the line back down the moor in hopes of picking up singles. Now that the excitement was over, my feet began to throb again. The cut on my hand was reasonably deep and might need a few stitches. My old Scott felt like a piece of field artillery.

"Come forward a bitee, please, Mr. Hummel."

Dick Hummel took a few faltering steps up to the line. He looked exhausted.

"A wee bitee to the right, Juan!" Ben shouted.

Then he leaned forward on his staff and raised himself ever so slightly onto his tiptoes. Turning his head to the right, he inspected that end of the line. Then, as if he had all the time in the world, he turned and looked down his left flank. Next, the gamekeeper focused his eyes forward, across the moor. For endless moments, he seemed lost in thought as if he might be planning strategy. This landscape, which, for him, gave up its clues, its hints of cover, food, and water, was, for me, only an endless expanse of heather.

I stood where I was, waiting patiently. The only sound was the wind whistling around the collar of my old shooting coat. The seconds ticked by like eons. Finally, the word came.

"On we go slowly," he called out.

32

The White Pheasant

Brian Robinson, my loader, slung my pair of O/Us over his shoulder with a grunt. "Ready, sir?" he asked. He was a ruddy-cheeked little Yorkshire man and the veteran of countless pheasant drives. It was my second day of shooting at Constable Burton.

"Yes, I'm ready," I said, noticing how small he looked under the weight of the two guns, my shell bag, and other paraphernalia.

"Here, Brian, I'll take that bag."

"Oh, no, sir," he said, refusing to give it to me.

"But, Brian ..."

"Coming, sir?" he asked stubbornly.

Okay, I give up, I thought.

He was old school, a stickler for protocol.

"So, the squire said something about white pheasants. What's that about?" I asked, walking along beside him.

"They're not to be shot, sir," he answered.

"I know, but what are they?"

"Well you'll see," he began, puffing under his load, "a pheasant in its normal plumage is beautifully camouflaged. In a covert, it's almost impossible to see."

"Yes," I said.

"So, the gamekeeper places a single white bird in each flock. White stands out very well. That's how he keeps track of them, by spotting that white pheasant."

"So, you're not supposed to shoot them."

"Oh, no sir, it's tradition. And there's a £100 fine if you do."

"You mean it's against the law?"

"No, it's just tradition. All the estates have it."

"So where does the money go?"

"To various charities. Here it goes to kidney research. You see the old gamekeeper, who was here for many years, died of kidney failure. He was quite loved here and about. So, it's given to kidney research in his honor."

What a beautiful gesture, I thought. I could see the old gent in his tweeds and cap puttering around the estate. He was probably long past usefulness but kept on by the squire out of love and respect. And now to have him honored in this way was enough to make an old shotgunner tear up.

"Watch your footing, sir," Brian said, waking me from my daydream.

We were crossing a shallow stream that crossed the lane. I went ahead as he had instructed and stood waiting on the far bank. But when I looked back, I found the little man struggling with the swift current and the weight of our gear.

"Let me help you, Brian?" I called.

"Oh, no. You just stay where you are, sir," he said, out of breath.

I felt like some indolent fop. I suddenly imagined myself standing there in a powdered wig and purple velvet jacket, perhaps sniffing a scented hanky as my manservant toiled under the burden of my shooting gear. Thankfully, he got across.

The current gamekeeper had already driven the pegs when we arrived. Brian and I found we were posted second from the left end of the line. The guns were stretched along a narrow dirt lane at the bottom of a hill. Ahead of us and up the slope was a kale field where the pheasants were holding.

The beaters had just started moving in when one of them shouted, "Partridge!"

I looked up the hill and saw a half-dozen plump gray missiles rocketing toward me. I had never shot a gray partridge. What had once been a mainstay of driven shooting in England had now become relatively rare in Yorkshire. An opportunity like this didn't often come along.

"Partridge, sir!" Brian shouted as he shoved one of my guns at me.

Fortunately, the birds were on us in an instant. I had no time to do anything but react instinctively. Too much thinking often works to my detriment. I swung the barrels just past a bird in the center of the group and squeezed the trigger. I didn't see him tumble. I only sensed it. Then swinging hard, I caught up with the last one just before it got out of range. This was a fine showing for me. I am, at best, an average wing shot.

"There's your left and right!" Brian said approvingly as if he were filling out a scorecard.

I wanted to pick up one of the birds and inspect it, but Brian stopped me. "The pickers-up will get them later, sir," he said, handing me the other gun.

The first pheasants had begun coming in from the kale field in front of us. I saw we weren't going to get the best of it. Most of the birds headed toward the center of the line. We were seeing very few shots. I was tempted to poach a bird or two off the gun to my left but thought better of it. Anyway, Brian wouldn't have allowed it. He was making a judgment call for every one that came near us.

"It's wide, sir," he called, warning me off a bird that rightfully belonged to the gun on my left.

"Too low, sir," he said of another that he didn't consider sporting.

There was a glaring sun, and the sky was hazy and chalk white. The pheasants appeared only as black silhouettes against the bright background. I heard the guns in the middle of the line cracking away, and it reminded me to put in my earplugs.

Then a single bird separated from the rest and came straight toward us. The shooting down the line grew more intense, and Brian said something to me, but I couldn't hear him. Did he say it's the right one? I could only see the dark form, the colorless silhouette of a pheasant like a target in a shooting gallery. I put the gun to my shoulder and swung the barrels, pushing them past the bird and blotting him out.

At that moment, in that fraction of a second, anything could have happened. The future was yet undetermined. I could have hesitated. I could have released the pressure on the trigger and let the bird go. What did Brian say? But I pulled the trigger, felt the jar against my shoulder and heard the report. It was done. It could never be changed. The pheasant was hit squarely. It folded high in the air and tumbled, hitting the ground ten or twelve feet behind me.

"Damn, what is that, Brian?" I asked. "Have I shot a freaking chicken?" It looked for all the world like a big white Leghorn rooster. There was silence.

Then Brian whispered, "You've shot a white one, sir."

As if on signal, the shooting down the line stopped. I could feel my face grow hot. It seemed the whole party had turned to stare. The thrill of having doubled on gray partridge was now a distant memory.

A voice inside me said, *Here you are thousands of miles from home, and you've gone and shot one of their sacred birds.*

The drive was over. Brian wordlessly picked up the pheasant, and we started back.

"But, Brian, what does it mean?" I asked.

"They're not to be shot, sir. It will be £100."

The fine stung me all right, but that was not the real source of my anguish. We hadn't gone far when we ran into the squire and his gamekeeper. The squire looked at the bird. "I'm afraid that's £100 for kidney research, old boy."

"Yes, well, of course," I answered. "Glad to pitch in and do my part for kidney research," I said.

At that moment, someone called to him from across the field. His attention was required elsewhere. He apologized, and he and the gamekeeper hurried away. I wasn't sure if he had been about to laugh or have me put in the dungeon. Two of the other guns intercepted us on the walk back. "Did you know it was a white one?" one of them asked.

"Well, no, there was the, uh, light and the glare and the noise and all. But I don't mind paying, really. It's for a worthy cause."

"Gosh, a white pheasant," the other observed. "That's a £100 fine, right?"

"Yes, well, um, happy to do my part for good old kidney research."

By then I was getting used to posing as a philanthropist. I had myself sounding downright noble. However, I was honest with Jenn. At lunch at the manor house, I told her about it.

"I shot a white pheasant," I said.

"What does that mean?" she asked.

"I'm not sure. All I know is I owe £100 to kidney research."

"Well, that's not such a terrible thing, is it?"

"I guess not. I just don't know how embarrassed I'm supposed to be."

That afternoon I felt as though the white pheasant was hanging around my neck like Melville's albatross. Was everyone staring? The guns were stretched along a small creek that ran through an open pasture. Brian and I had drawn No. 5 that morning, which, on this drive, put us near the center of the line. The birds were to be driven out of thick cover about 100 yards ahead of us.

On signal the beaters started through the woods. As they moved in deeper, groups of four to six birds took to the air. They came high and fast, and I got a fair number of shots. It was a good drive, but I didn't shoot particularly well. As I said, I'm an average shot, and most anything can throw me off. The ghost of that big white rooster was looming in my mind.

By dinnertime, my dark mood had really settled in. I sat quietly, hardly able to talk to the other guns and their wives.

"Are you still agonizing about that silly white pheasant?" Jenn asked.

"Of course not," I lied.

The group was especially raucous that night. Everyone was having a grand time. But, of course, they could enjoy themselves. None of them had murdered a sacred animal. After dinner, Jenn was deep in conversation with one of her new lady friends across the table. It had something to do with an antique boot scraper they'd seen at one of the local shops. I got up and slipped out.

We had the run of the place so I took a snifter of cognac and wandered up the hall. I found myself in the cavernous front parlor. The room was filled with portraits, photographs, and memorabilia, the trappings of a family who had owned the same plot of land for 1,000 years. But tonight, something was different. Or maybe it was just me. Could it be something I hadn't noticed before? Yes, there on the mantel, what was that? It was a mounted bird. It was a WHITE PHEASANT.

Suddenly, the squire was at my side.

"You mean you?" I asked.

"The buggers are hard to make out sometimes. Aren't they?"

"But I thought I was the only ..."

"Oh, no," he interrupted, "There are quite a few of us. In fact, we get together for dinner once a year in London. You should join us, old boy!"

"You mean there's some sort of club?" I asked.

"Oh, no, it's very informal, just lots of jokes and funny speeches," he said. "There are about fifty of us and all good chaps. But I must warn you," he said with a laugh, "it's the new fellow who picks up the tab for the evening."

I made quick mental calculations. Let's see, a minimum of $75 each for dinner and a glass or two of wine in some posh London restaurant. Then there would probably be cognac, espresso, and cigars afterward. And who knows how late a bunch of shotgun bums might stay? That's a minimum of, say, $5,000.

"I'll get back to you," I said.

It's been almost a year since that last trip to England. I am back at home now adding the last touches to this account. In my office, which doubles as a den, there is a lifetime of shooting memorabilia: souvenirs

BOB McDILL

of hunts in the rice fields of Arkansas, the mountains of Mexico, the prairies of Canada, and the moors of Scotland and England. There are prints, momentous, mounted birds, and pictures of shoots with companions now gone. But in a very prominent place on a table, which holds a clock that belonged to my grandfather along with a few leather-bound books, is a white pheasant. I had it mounted.

After all, I earned it. Shooting it cost me £100.

Did I learn anything from the experience? I could say that it taught me the foolishness of haste and the wisdom of caution. But when I look at that big snow white bird, it occurs to me that I might have disregarded another more obvious lesson: Excellence is a lonely pursuit, but when you do something stupid, you've always got company.

INDEX

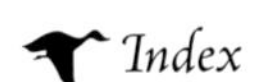

Names and Email Addresses of Artists

Alan Phillips	alanlovesart@aol.com
Bob White	bobwhitestudio.com